Naoiya's Quick Comforts

To my fluffy-sock-wearing comfort-seeker, Maryam.

Let us soothe our bodies and minds through the warmth and the familiarity of food.

Nadiya's Quick Comforts

Over 80 recipes designed to be
made quickly & eaten slowly.

Nadiya Hussain

Photography By Chris Terry

Contents

Introduction	6-9
Cooking Pot	10-37
Frying Pan	38-71
Roasting Dish	72-93
Air Fryer	94-119
Tray Bakes	120-145
Deep Fried	146-173
Cake Tin	174-205
Chocolate	206-229
Thanks	230-231
Index	232-239

Introduction

What does comfort mean to me? When I hear the word comfort, I think of warmth. Of safety and familiarity. These are precious feelings and that is why I wanted to gather together a collection of recipes that bring comfort to my heart as well as my belly.

I am all about comfort food! What purpose does food serve, if it doesn't make you happy? Food is meant to bring joy, whether you are making it, eating it, or both.

Sometimes the only thing that can heal a sad face, a weary heart, tired feet and teary eyes is comfort food. A plate or a meal that heals you from the outside in and says I love you.

But what comfort doesn't have to do is eat into our precious time. We can still make and enjoy delicious food that has the power to heal, but without spending hours in the kitchen.

Every recipe in this book is designed to be made quickly and eaten slowly. There are six chapters devised around a single style of cooking, in which the same piece of equipment is used for every recipe: a frying pan chapter, a cooking pot chapter, a roasting dish chapter, an oven tray chapter, a cake tin chapter and an air fryer chapter. These chapters are designed and written to make your life easier. Decide what receptacle you want to cook in and discover a whole chapter filled with delicious comforting recipes for you to pick from.

There are also two other very special chapters. One is the chocolate chapter, because, I ask you, can there truly be comfort without chocolate? I think not. And finally, my absolute favourite chapter, the deep-frying chapter, because I have never deep fried anything that hasn't tasted absolutely dynamite delicious!

In a world that too often promotes restriction and giving up things that make us deeply happy, let's do the opposite. Let's embrace comfort, let's celebrate food that makes us feel good and let's do it with time to spare.

Nadiya x

'What does *comfort* mean to me? When I hear the word *comfort*, I think of warmth. Of safety and familiarity. These are precious feelings and that is why I wanted to gather together a collection of recipes that bring comfort to my heart as well as my belly.'

Cooking Pot

Onions make a great base for a sauce, but when cooked well they can also <u>be</u> the sauce. Here, the onions are cooked until soft and golden, laced with garlic and thyme and blended until smooth. So simple but so delicious.

Caramelized Onion Pasta

SERVES 4

500g fusilli pasta
4 tbsp vegetable oil
8 cloves of garlic, sliced
4 medium onions, peeled and thinly sliced
2 tsp salt
1 tsp sugar
1 tbsp dried thyme

To serve
chilli flakes
green salad
garlic bread

1. Start by cooking the fusilli as per the packet instructions. Boil and drain in a colander, but make sure to reserve 200ml of the cooking water.
2. Run the pasta under cold water, to stop it sticking, and set aside.
3. To the same pan, add the vegetable oil and heat on a medium heat.
4. Add the garlic and cook until really golden brown.
5. Now add the sliced onions, along with the salt, sugar and dried thyme, and cook until the onions are soft and golden brown.
6. Pop the mixture into a blender along with the reserved cooking water and blend to a smooth paste.
7. Put the sauce back into the pan, add the pasta and warm it through in the hot sauce.
8. Serve, sprinkled with chilli flakes, alongside a green salad and some garlic bread.

Cook: 35 Mins
Prep: 12 Mins

Everyone needs to know how to make a simple dhal, so I am going to show you. If you love lentils, you will adore this. If you don't like lentils, I think you will, after this. Made with delicate flavours and a kick of garlic, this is the perfect dhal.

Simple Dhal

SERVES 4

- 100ml vegetable oil
- 10 cloves of garlic, thinly sliced
- 1 medium onion, thinly sliced
- 2 x 400g tins of brown/green lentils
- 500ml of cold water
- 1 bay leaf
- 1 large dried red chilli
- 2 tsp salt
- 1 tsp ground turmeric
- a small handful of fresh coriander, thinly sliced

To serve
- microwave rice
- naan bread
- lemon wedges

1. Put a pan on the hob on a high heat. Add the oil, and as soon as it's hot, add the garlic and fry until it's a deep golden brown.
2. Add the onions and cook on a high heat until golden.
3. Pour the tinned lentils into the pan, no need to drain.
4. Now add the water, bay leaf, dried red chilli, salt and turmeric.
5. Bring to the boil and leave to simmer until the water has almost evaporated and the mixture has thickened.
6. Take off the heat and sprinkle over the coriander.
7. Serve with rice, naan bread and lemon wedges.

Cook: 35 Mins
Prep: 14 Mins

Soba noodles are an all-round favourite in our home and perfect for a noodle soup dish like this. The broth is aromatic and healing. Best of all, unlike traditional broths, this is my fast version, without compromising on flavour.

Soba Chicken Noodles

SERVES 4

1 litre cold water
4 chicken stock cubes
1 clementine, halved
1 large stick of cinnamon
1 star anise
100ml soy sauce
500g boneless chicken thighs, cut into strips
250g soba noodles
2 tsp ginger paste
2 tsp garlic paste
2 tsp chilli flakes
fresh coriander, finely chopped

To serve
lime wedges

1. Pour the of cold water into a pan and add the chicken stock cubes, halved clementine, stick of cinnamon, star anise, soy sauce and the boneless chicken thigh strips.

2. Bring everything to the boil and leave to simmer for 15 minutes.

3. Drain into a colander suspended over a bowl so you can catch all that liquid. Pour the liquid back into the pan.

4. Take out all the chicken strips from the colander and get rid of the rest of the stuff.

5. Add the soba noodles, ginger paste, garlic paste and chilli flakes and bring back to the boil, then simmer until the noodles are cooked.

6. Sprinkle over the coriander and serve with lime wedges.

{ Cook: 28 Mins   { Prep: 10 Mins

Meatballs are so versatile and can be eaten in so many different ways. These don't need to be fried separately. Everything is cooked in the spiced sauce, and the meatballs absorb all that delicious flavour.

Masala Meatballs

SERVES 4

For the sauce
5 tbsp vegetable oil
2 tbsp garlic paste
2 tbsp ginger paste
2 medium onions, peeled and roughly chopped
3 tbsp tomato purée
2 tsp salt
3 tbsp garam masala
200ml water

For the meatballs
500g lamb mince
1 tsp salt
1 tbsp garlic paste
1 tbsp garam masala

To serve
fresh coriander, finely chopped
microwave rice

1. Start by putting a pan on the hob on a high heat.
2. Pour in the vegetable oil, and as soon as it's hot, add the garlic paste and ginger paste and cook for a few minutes.
3. Put the onions and tomato paste into a blender with a small splash of water and blend to a smooth paste.
4. Add the onion/tomato mix to the pan along with the salt and cook for a few minutes, until some of the moisture has evaporated and the onions start to look drier.
5. Add the garam masala and water and leave to simmer away on a low to medium heat.
6. Meanwhile, put the lamb mince into a bowl and add the salt, garlic paste and garam masala. Get your hands in and mix everything together.
7. Make small balls and drop them all gently into the pan of simmering sauce. Give the pan a swirl occasionally to help the balls cook on all sides.
8. Leave to simmer uncovered for 20 minutes.
9. Sprinkle with chopped coriander and serve with rice.

{ Cook: 40 Mins   { Prep: 12 Mins

Sometimes all I want is chicken and rice, that's it, nothing else. And there is nothing wrong with that! So if you sometimes feel the same, try this recipe out. This dish is hearty, wholesome and packed with flavour.

Chicken Rice

SERVES 4

6 tbsp vegetable oil, plus a little extra

2 boneless chicken breasts, thinly sliced

500g basmati rice, washed until the water runs clear, and drained

2 tbsp Marmite

2 chicken stock cubes

100ml dark soy sauce

3 tbsp onion granules

750ml boiling water

To serve
kimchi

1. Put the oil into a large pan and get it really hot.
2. Add the sliced chicken and cook until it is golden brown, and any moisture that has come out of the chicken has evaporated.
3. Take the chicken out of the pan and set aside on a plate.
4. Add another splash of oil and your drained rice.
5. Cook the rice for a few minutes, stirring, then add the Marmite, stock cubes, soy sauce and onion granules and mix everything together.
6. Pour in the boiling water and cook the rice until all the water has been absorbed, stirring occasionally so it doesn't stick to the base of the pan.
7. Put the chicken on top of the rice, then put the lid on the pan and leave to steam on a low heat for 15 minutes.
8. Take the lid off and stir the chicken into the rice.
9. Serve with kimchi on the side.

{ Cook: 40 Mins   { Prep: 10 Mins

I love seafood, but I particularly love prawns, and this Creole-style recipe is packed with onion, garlic, celery, thyme and tomatoes. Prawns cook quickly, so this is fast and delicious.

Creole-style Prawns

SERVES 4

4 tbsp oil

6 cloves of garlic, finely chopped

2 sticks of celery, diced

1 medium onion, diced

1 green pepper, diced

2 tbsp dried thyme

1 tbsp ground coriander

2 tsp salt

1 x 400g jar of passata

2 x 400g packs of raw tiger prawns, defrosted

To serve
microwave rice

1. Put a pan on the stove on a medium to high heat.
2. Add the oil, and as soon as it's hot, add the garlic and fry until golden.
3. Add the celery, onion and pepper and cook until soft.
4. Now add the thyme, coriander and salt, and cook through for a few minutes.
5. Pour in the passata and cook for a few minutes more to allow everything to combine.
6. Add the prawns and cook for 10 minutes with the lid off.
7. Serve with rice.

Cook: 30 Mins **Prep:** 15 Mins

I love a fish curry; I grew up on the stuff. Over the years I've learned to make it in lots of different ways. This version is rich and creamy and packed with coconut flavour. The addition of cashew nuts makes it extra special.

Fish & Coconut Curry

SERVES 4

3 tbsp vegetable oil
100g whole cashews
2 tsp garlic paste
2 tsp ginger paste
2 medium onion, peeled and blended to a smooth paste
1 tsp salt
½ tsp ground turmeric
1 tsp paprika
3 tsp curry powder
1 x 400ml tin of coconut milk
400ml water
150g mangetout
80g baby spinach leaves
2 x 280g pieces of cod, cut into chunks

To serve
microwave rice
20g desiccated coconut, toasted
a small handful of fresh coriander, chopped
1 tsp chilli flakes

1. Put a 5-litre pot on the stove on a medium heat.
2. Add the vegetable oil to the pot, and when the oil is hot, add the cashews and toast until golden. Now add the garlic and ginger paste, along with the onion paste from the blender.
3. Add the salt and cook for a few minutes, until the onions are just golden brown.
4. Add the turmeric, paprika and curry powder and cook for a few minutes. If the onion starts to stick, add a small splash of water.
5. Pour in the coconut milk, then use the empty can to measure out the 400ml of water and pour that in too. Bring to the boil and cook on a high heat for 5 minutes.
6. Add the mangetout, spinach leaves and cod chunks and cook on a medium heat for 15 minutes with the lid off.
7. Serve with rice, and sprinkle with toasted coconut, chopped coriander and chilli flakes.

Cook: 35 Mins **Prep: 15 Mins**

Keema rice is a staple one-pot dish. Simply spiced mince cooked with rice all in the same pot, it's the kind of dish you will be serving up more than once a week.

Keema Rice

SERVES 4

5 tbsp vegetable oil
500g beef mince
1 tbsp ginger paste
1 tbsp garlic paste
1 tbsp salt
5 tbsp garam masala
500g basmati rice, washed until the water runs clear, and drained
750ml boiling water
300g frozen peas

To serve
yoghurt

1. Put a pan on the hob on a high heat.
2. Pour in the oil, and as soon as it's hot, add the beef mince and cook until browned.
3. Add the ginger paste, garlic paste and salt, and fry until all the moisture in the base of the pan has evaporated.
4. Add the garam masala and the basmati rice, and fry for 2 minutes, mixing everything together.
5. Pour in the boiling water and stir until combined. Keep mixing and cooking the rice on a high heat until all the water has been absorbed.
6. As soon as all the moisture has gone, layer the peas on top.
7. Put the lid on, lower the heat completely and leave to steam for 15 minutes.
8. Fluff up the rice and it is ready to serve, with a dollop of yoghurt on the side.

{ Cook: 45 Mins   { Prep: 7 Mins

I think onions get unfairly overlooked as a main ingredient. But let me tell you that onions make a great curry. This is sweet and creamy and so good with naan.

Garlicky Onion & Yoghurt Curry

SERVES 4

5 tbsp vegetable oil

15 cloves of garlic, finely chopped

5 medium onions, peeled and thinly sliced

2 tsp salt

½ tsp ground turmeric

1 tsp chilli powder

3 tsp ground coriander

1 lemon, juice only

300g Greek yoghurt

a small handful of fresh coriander, finely chopped

To serve
naan bread

1. Start by putting a pot on the hob. Add the oil and bring to a medium heat.
2. As soon as the oil is hot, add the garlic and cook until golden brown.
3. Now add all the onions, along with the salt, turmeric, chilli powder, ground coriander and lemon juice. Cook until the onions are soft and wilted.
4. As soon as the moisture has evaporated, add the yoghurt and cook for a few minutes.
5. Take off the heat and sprinkle over the coriander, then serve with some naan bread on the side.

Cook: 30 Mins **Prep:** 15 Mins

Tteokbokki is a Korean dish of chewy rice tubes which are often cooked in a stew. They are not always easy to find, but I love them, so I made my own version using rice paper, which is easy to find. These are spiced and flavourful and so much fun to eat.

Rice Paper Tteokbokki

MAKES 12

1 x 134g pack of rice paper spring roll wrappers
3 tbsp oil
6 cloves of garlic, finely chopped
750ml cold water
3 tbsp gochujang paste
2 tbsp soy sauce

To serve
sesame oil
spring onions, thinly sliced
sesame seeds

1. Dunk each sheet of rice paper into a plate of cold water and submerge it till soft.
2. As soon as each one is soft, roll it into a long log, cut it in half and set aside.
3. Add the oil to the pan, and when it's hot, add the chopped garlic. As soon as the garlic is brown, add the cold water, gochujang paste and soy sauce and boil for 5 minutes.
4. Add the rice paper rolls to the pan and cook for 5–8 minutes, until the rolls are coloured and soft and the liquid has thickened.
5. Serve with a drizzle of sesame oil and sprinkled with spring onions and sesame seeds.

photo overleaf

Cook: 20 Mins
Prep: 7 Mins

Rice Paper Tteokbokki

Rice pudding can be made in all manner of ways and every family has its own version. Mine uses basmati rice, which is aromatic, and I like to make it with spices like cinnamon and cardamom, finished with a little rose extract and topped with pistachios.

Rice Pudding

SERVES 4

2 litres whole milk
15 cardamom pods
2 tsp ground cinnamon
100g basmati rice
150g caster sugar
200ml double cream
½ tsp rose extract
pistachios, roughly chopped
raisins

1. Start by putting the milk into a pan.
2. Crush the cardamom pods and remove the black seeds from inside the husks, then grind the black seeds down to a fine powder. Add to the milk.
3. Add the ground cinnamon, then put the pan on the hob and bring the milk to the boil.
4. Put your basmati rice into a blender and blend it down to very small pieces, without reducing it to a powder.
5. Add the rice to the milk and bring to the boil, then leave to simmer on a medium heat for 20-25 minutes, making sure to stir every now and again.
6. As soon as the mixture has thickened, add the caster sugar and double cream, along with the rose extract, and mix through.
7. You can serve this hot straight away, with pistachios and raisins sprinkled on the top. It's also great served chilled.

Cook: 35 Mins
Prep: 7 Mins

Dumplings are like a hug for your insides. Made with a buttery golden syrup sauce, these are tender, sweet and a perfect go-to pudding.

Golden Syrup Dumplings

SERVES 4

For the syrup
30g butter
165g soft brown sugar
125ml golden syrup
375ml water
a large pinch of salt

For the dumplings
185g self-raising flour
30g butter
80ml golden syrup
80ml whole milk

To serve
pouring cream or ice cream

1. Start by making the syrup.
2. Put a pan on the hob on a medium to low heat.
3. Add the butter, soft brown sugar, golden syrup, water and salt, and bring the mixture to the boil, stirring to make sure the sugar dissolves.
4. As soon as the sugar dissolves, turn the heat down as low as possible and get on to making the dumplings.
5. Put the self-raising flour into a bowl with the butter and golden syrup.
6. Use your fingertips to rub the butter and golden syrup into the flour – when you are left with a lumpy crumb, pour in the milk and use a spoon to bring the dough together.
7. Drop 1 tablespoon of the dough at a time into the syrup, until you have added all the dough in one even layer.
8. Leave to simmer on a low heat, with the lid on, for 25 minutes until the top layer is cooked.
9. Serve the dumplings and syrup hot, with pouring cream or ice cream.

photo overleaf

Cook: 45 Mins
Prep: 8 Mins

Golden Syrup Dumplings

Frying Pan

Stir-fries are a go-to in our house. They don't have to be complicated or laborious. This is the perfect balance of ginger and beef and is a total hit every time.

Beef Ginger Stir-fry

SERVES 4

500g diced beef, thinly sliced

3 tbsp cornflour

3 tbsp water

vegetable oil, for frying

1 tbsp coriander seeds, lightly crushed

1 tbsp chilli flakes

4 cloves of garlic, peeled and thinly sliced

1 tsp salt

300g tenderstem broccoli, cut into 2cm pieces

200g green beans, cut into 2cm pieces

200g baby corn, cut into 2cm pieces

3 tbsp apple cider vinegar

2 tbsp runny honey

1 tbsp ground ginger

1 red onion, peeled and thinly sliced

8cm ginger, peeled and cut into thin strips

a small handful of fresh coriander, finely chopped

To serve
microwave sticky white rice

1. Put the thinly sliced beef into a bowl. Stir the cornflour into the water, then add to the bowl and mix until you have an even coating around the beef.

2. Add a drizzle of oil to the pan and put it on a medium heat. As soon as the oil is hot, add the beef and fry until browned all over.

3. Take the beef out of the pan and set aside on a plate.

4. Add a little more oil to the pan if you need to. Then add the coriander seeds, chilli flakes and garlic, and fry until the garlic is golden.

5. Now add the salt, along with the tenderstem broccoli, green beans and baby corn, and cook until just steamed and slightly softened.

6. Mix the apple cider vinegar, runny honey and ground ginger in a small bowl.

7. Put the beef back into the pan, along with the vinegar and honey mixture, and stir to warm the beef through.

8. Stir in the red onion, then take off the heat.

9. Serve with the strips of ginger and a sprinkling of fresh coriander and some sticky white rice.

Cook: 35 Mins   Prep: 24 Mins

If cheese and pickles are your thing, then this is absolutely your thing. Salty pickle, wrapped in a toasted crisp slice of cheesy deliciousness! What else is there to say?

Cheese and Pickle Snack

MAKES 5

5 slices of mature Cheddar cheese

5 pickle spears, drained and patted dry

To serve
sour cream

1. Heat a non-stick pan on the hob, on a high heat. Have a plate ready with some kitchen paper.

2. Lay your cheese slices in the pan and fry on a high heat until golden brown all over. The cheese will crisp up around the edges and bubble all over.

3. Carefully take the cheese out and lay it on the kitchen paper.

4. As soon as the cheese starts to cool, put a pickle in the centre of each one and wrap the pickle in the cheese.

5. Remove to a serving plate, giving the cheese some time to cool and crisp up.

6. Serve with sour cream and enjoy.

Cook: 15 Mins
Prep: 5 Mins

I'm a big fan of cabbage and I don't think people cook with it enough. So this is a great way of using it to make a simple cabbage pancake, which I like to serve topped with tuna and is really moreish to eat.

Cabbage Tuna Pancake

MAKES 4

- 200g white cabbage, shredded in a processor until very fine
- 3 medium eggs
- ½ tsp salt
- 1 tsp black pepper
- 6 tbsp vegetable oil
- 1 x 145g can of tuna, drained
- 4 tbsp mayonnaise
- 1 tsp cayenne pepper
- 1 large spring onion, thinly sliced
- sriracha sauce

1. Put the shredded cabbage into a bowl along with the eggs, salt and black pepper, and whisk using a fork for about 5 minutes, until the mixture is frothy.
2. Put a frying pan on a medium heat and add the oil.
3. As soon as the oil is hot, pour in the cabbage mixture and flatten out.
4. Fry until golden and crisp on the base, then put the pan under the grill for a few minutes to crisp up the top.
5. Put the canned tuna, mayonnaise, cayenne pepper and spring onion into a bowl and mix together.
6. Slide the pancake on to a board or a plate, top it with the tuna, drizzle over sriracha, and serve cut into quarters.

photo overleaf

Cook: 16 Mins

Prep: 10 Mins

Cabbage Tuna Pancake

I use a lot of rice paper and always have plenty at home, as it can be used in a wide variety of different ways. Rice paper fried is delicious, as are most things that are fried! These are filled with an aromatic chicken mince.

Chicken Half-moons

MAKES 6

500g chicken mince
1 tsp garlic paste
1 tsp ginger paste
2 spring onions, thinly sliced
1 tsp salt
3 tsp chilli flakes
1 medium egg
6 rice paper circles
vegetable oil, for frying

To serve
hot sauce

1. Start by putting the chicken mince into a bowl.
2. Add the garlic paste and ginger paste along with the sliced spring onions, salt and chilli flakes.
3. Add the egg and mix until everything is really well combined.
4. Get a plate with sides and pour in some cold water.
5. Dunk a rice paper sheet into the water and soak until soft – this will only take a few seconds.
6. Place the paper on a board, add a sixth of the mixture to one half of the paper, and spread out thinly, leaving a border of 1cm. Fold the other half over, then fold the border back over the half-moon to seal.
7. Do the same to the other five.
8. Pour some oil into the base of your frying pan so that it is entirely covered.
9. Heat the oil on a high heat and when it's hot, gently lower the half-moons in, two at a time, and fry until crisp and golden. After a few minutes, gently flip them over so they are cooked on both sides. Repeat until they are all done.
10. Serve with a side of your favourite hot sauce.

photo overleaf

Cook: 26 Mins
Prep: 8 Mins

Chicken Half-moons

As a family of rice eaters, we always have rice left over. No one is ever fed up with the things that I make using leftovers, and fried rice is no exception. This rice is mixed with crab sticks, which give it a great texture, colour and flavour.

Crab Stick Fried Rice

SERVES 4

- 6 tbsp vegetable oil
- 1 tsp garlic paste
- 2 medium onions, peeled and diced
- 1 tsp salt
- ½ tsp ground turmeric
- ½ tsp chilli powder
- 1 x 198g tin of sweetcorn, drained
- 2 packets of microwave rice
- 1 x 120g pack of crab sticks, chopped into chunks
- a small handful of fresh coriander

To serve
frilly fried eggs

1. Start by putting the pan on the hob on a high to medium heat.
2. Add the oil, and as soon as it's hot, add the garlic paste and cook for a minute.
3. Now add the onions and salt, and fry for a few minutes until the onion is lovely and soft.
4. Add the turmeric, chilli powder and drained sweetcorn, and fry until there is no liquid left in the base of the pan.
5. Open the rice and tip into the pan, using a wooden spoon to break the grains apart. Add a splash of water and fry until the rice has heated through.
6. Stir in the crab sticks and fry on a high heat so that some of the rice sticks and colours a little. Stir in the fresh coriander.
7. Take off the heat and serve each portion with a crispy frilly fried egg.

Cook: 20 Mins
Prep: 15 Mins

Potato salad is my go-to in the summer and as a side when I am cooking through the year. But I like to find new ways of making it each time. With this potato salad you don't even have to boil and peel any potatoes, because we are using hash browns. And for added crunch, we are frying up some noodles, to really make it different!

Crunchy Noodle Potato Salad

SERVES 4–6

- 3 tbsp vegetable oil
- 225g egg noodles
- 350g frozen hash browns
- 1 red onions, peeled and sliced
- 2 green chillies, thinly sliced
- a large handful of fresh coriander, thinly sliced
- 1 tsp salt, plus extra for the noodles
- 6 tbsp mayonnaise
- 4 tbsp brown sauce
- juice of ½ a lemon
- 1 tbsp ground coriander

1. Put your frying pan on the hob and add enough oil to cover the entire base of the pan. As soon as the oil is hot, break in the noodles and fry until golden brown. You may have to do this in batches.
2. Using a slotted spoon, remove the fried noodles on to a plate lined with kitchen paper. Sprinkle with salt and set aside.
3. Now break in pieces of the hash browns and fry on a high heat, till crispy and golden. Set aside and leave to cool.
4. Put the sliced red onion, green chillies, fresh coriander and salt into a bowl.
5. Put the mayonnaise, brown sauce, lemon juice and ground coriander into a smaller bowl and mix together. Add to the bowl of red onion and chillies and mix through.
6. Add the fried hash browns and mix.
7. Transfer to a serving dish, sprinkle over the noodles and serve.

Cook: 45 Mins
Prep: 16 Mins

If I'm making a salad, one thing I can promise is that it won't be cold and insipid. It will be warm, it will be vibrant and it will be filling. This salad ticks all those boxes. Dumplings not only bring flavour and texture, but also make the whole thing into a proper meal.

Dumpling Salad

SERVES 4

- 3 tbsp oil
- 20 frozen veg gyoza
- 6 tbsp dark soy sauce
- 3 tbsp apple cider vinegar
- 2 tbsp sesame oil
- 2 tbsp runny honey
- 4 cloves of garlic
- 2 tsp chilli flakes
- 1 red onion, peeled and thinly sliced
- 1 whole cucumber, halved lengthways and centre seeds removed, sliced into 1cm half-moons
- A small handful of fresh coriander, finely chopped
- sesame seeds

1. Put the oil into a lidded frying pan and bring to a high heat.
2. Add the frozen veg gyoza one by one, and as soon as you have them all in the pan, cook with the lid on until they are crispy on the base and steamed inside. This can take about 6–8 minutes.
3. Once the gyoza are cooked, set them aside in the pan with the lid off.
4. Put the dark soy sauce, apple cider vinegar, sesame oil and runny honey into a large bowl.
5. Grate your garlic cloves into the mixture.
6. Add the chilli flakes and give everything a really good mix.
7. Add the sliced red onion and the cucumber half-moons. Mix everything through, then add your dumplings and mix until well combined.
8. To finish, sprinkle over the fresh coriander and sesame seeds and the salad is ready to eat.

Cook: 15 Mins
Prep: 15 Mins

No one in my house likes feta but me, so I always make these just for myself and freeze a few. Filled with salty feta, tangy sun-dried tomatoes, with a hint of cumin and spinach, they are fried in a pan to get them really crispy on the outside.

Filo Feta Squares

MAKES 7

vegetable oil

7 sheets of filo pastry

80g spinach, thinly sliced

200g feta

8 sun-dried tomatoes, chopped

2 tsp ground cumin

runny honey

To serve
garlic mayonnaise

1. Start by preparing the filo sheets: brush each sheet with oil and fold in half.
2. Divide the spinach between the 7 filo sheets.
3. Crumble some of the feta over each sheet.
4. Now sprinkle on the chopped sun-dried tomatoes.
5. Sprinkle on the ground cumin and drizzle on some honey.
6. Brush the edges with a little more oil. Fold the filo over to encase the filling – you should be left with a rectangle. Fold over the excess to make neat squares.
7. Put a frying pan on the hob and add a drizzle of oil.
8. As soon as the oil is hot, put the parcels in and fry until deep golden brown on both sides.
9. Serve with garlic mayonnaise.

Cook: 28 Mins

Prep: 8 Mins

Udon are my favourite noodles. I love how substantial they are and I really enjoy the chew of them. So if I'm making noodles, expect udon! These are packed with flavour and taste even better the next day, if there are any left.

Honey Chicken Udon

SERVES 4

- 500g chicken thighs, cut into thin strips
- 2 tbsp cornflour
- 2 tbsp water
- 5 tbsp vegetable oil
- 3 tsp chilli flakes
- 5 cloves of garlic, grated
- 100ml soy sauce
- 2 tbsp runny honey
- 1 lime, juice only
- 4 x 150g packs of pre-cooked udon noodles
- 300g fresh beansprouts
- 3 spring onions, cut into 5cm strips

To serve
- sesame seeds
- a small handful of fresh coriander, finely chopped

1. Put the chicken strips into a large bowl. Mix the cornflour into the water, add to the bowl and mix until everything is completely combined.
2. Put the oil into your frying pan, and when it's hot, cook the chicken in two batches, until cooked through and golden brown, then remove the chicken from the pan and keep it warm.
3. Now add a little extra oil into the pan if you need to. Add the chilli flakes and allow some of that red colour to seep out.
4. Now add the grated garlic and fry until golden.
5. Pour in the soy sauce, honey and lime juice.
6. Add the noodles, beansprouts and spring onions, return the chicken to the pan and mix really well until everything is coated.
7. Serve with a generous sprinkling of sesame seeds and fresh coriander.

Cook: 30 Mins
Prep: 15 Mins

Here's another great gnocchi recipe to prove to you that it doesn't have to be boiled (see also page 111). I prefer it when it has a bit of a crunch to it, and fried gnocchi is sensational. This is simply fried with garlic, onion, spinach and black pepper. It will change how you enjoy gnocchi, in a good way.

Pan-fried Gnocchi

SERVES 4

- 5 tbsp vegetable oil, for frying
- 2 x 280g packets of gnocchi
- 3 cloves of garlic, grated
- 1 medium onion, peeled and sliced
- 1 tsp salt
- 2 tsp ground black pepper
- 1 red pepper, sliced
- 80g spinach
- 3 tbsp chilli sauce
- 50g Parmesan cheese, grated

1. Put your frying pan on the hob on a medium to high heat. Add a couple of tablespoons of oil to the pan, then add the gnocchi and fry until golden on all sides.
2. Take the gnocchi out of the pan and set aside.
3. Add a splash more oil to the pan, then add the garlic and fry until golden.
4. Add the onion, salt, black pepper and red pepper, and cook until the red peppers have just softened.
5. Now put the gnocchi back into the pan with the spinach and a splash of water, and cook until the spinach has wilted and there isn't any liquid left in the base of the pan.
6. Take off the heat, drizzle with chilli sauce and sprinkle over the Parmesan cheese.
7. Put under the grill for just a few minutes, to crisp up the cheese, and it's ready to eat.

Cook: 40 Mins
Prep: 10 Mins

I love making pancakes, but I don't always love being at the stove flipping pancakes for what can sometimes feel like an age. So these are the answer! We make the batter and fry the whole lot in one go, stirring it up to make the most scrummy nibbles. Sprinkled with cinnamon sugar, these are great for sharing and great for the morning after a sleepover.

Pancake Nibbles

SERVES 4–6

For the batter
250g self-raising flour
2 tsp baking powder
3 tbsp caster sugar
2 medium eggs
300ml whole milk
1 tsp vanilla extract
1 tsp almond extract
a pinch of salt
150g butter

For the cinnamon sprinkle
150g caster sugar
2 tsp ground cinnamon

To serve
yoghurt
berries

1. Start by making the batter. Put the self-raising flour into a bowl with the baking powder and caster sugar and whisk together to combine well.

2. Now add the eggs, whole milk, vanilla and almond extracts along with the salt, and whisk until you have a smooth, thick batter.

3. Set aside and begin to brown the butter.

4. Put a large non-stick frying pan on the hob on a high heat. Add the butter to the pan and let it melt.

5. Brown the butter by allowing it to become frothy – you should see the milk solids turning a golden brown and the aroma should be nutty.

6. Pour all the batter into the pan and allow it to fry in one entire piece. As soon as you can see the underside is cooked, get a spatula in there and start to break up pieces of the batter and flip them.

7. Keep mixing until you have pancake nibbles that are cooked and firm.

8. Put the nibbles on a serving plate. Mix the caster sugar and cinnamon in a small bowl. Sprinkle the sugar all over the nibbles and toss through, using a spoon.

9. They are ready to serve and enjoy, with some yoghurt and berries if you like.

{ Cook: 26 Mins
{ Prep: 12 Mins

To me, toasties are a whole entire love language. And with these, think prawn toast, but as a toastie! Now all you have to do is make them and enjoy the magic of these toasties, with their succulent filling and crisp fried exterior.

Prawn Toasties

MAKES 3

200g raw prawns, defrosted

1 tbsp cornflour

3 cloves of garlic

1 spring onion, thinly sliced

2 tsp cumin seeds

½ tsp salt

6 thick slices of white bread

vegetable oil, for frying

To serve
sweet chilli sauce

1. Put the raw prawns into a food processor with the cornflour and garlic and blend to a smooth paste.
2. Put the paste into a bowl with the sliced spring onion, cumin seeds and salt, and mix well.
3. Divide the mixture equally between 3 slices of bread, making sure to spread it all the way to the sides.
4. Sandwich with a second piece of bread, push together firmly and set aside.
5. Put a pan on the hob and add the vegetable oil to come about ½cm up the sides. Heat the oil to a medium heat.
6. As soon as the oil is hot, put 2 of the sandwiches into the pan and fry on each side until golden brown – this should take about 3–4 minutes.
7. Drain on a plate lined with kitchen paper.
8. Fry the last sandwich, then cut them all into triangles, and they are ready to eat, dipped into some sweet chilli sauce.

{ **Cook:** 20 Mins   { **Prep:** 10 Mins

Crumpets are not just for butter and jam. Crumpets can be enjoyed savoury too. These are fried with onions and chillies and are bound together with cooked eggs. They are so good, I don't know if you will ever put butter and jam on your crumpets again.

Savoury Crumpets

SERVES 4

- 6 tbsp vegetable oil
- 2 medium onions, peeled and thinly sliced
- 3 small green chillies, thinly sliced
- 1 tsp salt, plus an extra pinch for the eggs
- 6 crumpets, cubed
- 6 medium eggs
- a small handful of fresh coriander, finely chopped

1. Start by adding the oil to your frying pan, and when it's hot, add the sliced onions and cook until they are soft.
2. Add the green chillies and salt.
3. Add the cubed crumpets and cook until they are warmed through and toasted.
4. Put the eggs into a bowl with a pinch of salt and mix to combine.
5. Pour the eggs all over the crumpets in the pan and cook until the egg is no longer runny. Make sure to mix and break up the mixture as you go.
6. As soon as the egg is cooked through, sprinkle over the coriander and serve in bowls.

photos overleaf

Cook: 30 Mins
Prep: 16 Mins

Savoury Crumpets

Steak and mushroom is a match made in heaven and beyond. This is a simple one-pan steak dinner that you won't even break a sweat for. Creamy and earthy, it's the perfect midweek meal after a long day at work.

Steak and Mushroom

SERVES 4

4 tbsp vegetable oil

600g steak, thinly sliced

4 cloves of garlic, grated

1 tsp salt

3 tbsp cracked black pepper

300g mushrooms, quartered

2 tbsp apple cider vinegar

300ml double cream

a large handful of parsley, chopped

cayenne pepper, to sprinkle

To serve
microwave creamy mash

1. Put the frying pan on the hob on a medium to high heat.
2. Add the oil to the pan, and as soon as it's hot, add the steak and fry in two batches until browned. Set aside on a plate.
3. Add the grated garlic to the pan and fry until golden.
4. Now add the salt, black pepper and mushrooms. Cook until there is no more liquid in the pan and the mushrooms are soft.
5. Drizzle in the apple cider vinegar and double cream and cook until you have a nice thick sauce.
6. Return the steak to the pan and mix together.
7. Sprinkle over the fresh parsley and cayenne pepper, and serve with hot mash.

Cook: 40 Mins **Prep:** 15 Mins

Roasting Dish

Salty feta and sweet cherry tomatoes, all baked with pasta in a roasting dish. Simplest dinner yet.

Baked Feta Pasta

SERVES 4

- 100ml vegetable oil
- 300g cherry tomatoes
- 200g feta cheese
- 1 tsp salt
- 1 tsp dried basil
- 1 tsp onion granules
- 1 tsp garlic granules
- 1 tsp dried rosemary
- 1 tsp dried oregano
- 1 tsp dried thyme
- 1 tbsp cornflour
- 500g fusilli pasta
- 450-500ml boiling water

To serve
garlic bread

1. Preheat the oven to 200°C fan.
2. Put the vegetable oil into a 25 x 35cm roasting dish, then add the cherry tomatoes, and crumble in the feta cheese.
3. Put the salt, dried basil, onion granules, garlic granules, rosemary, oregano, thyme and cornflour into a small bowl. Mix really well, then add to the roasting dish and mix in.
4. Add the fusilli and the boiling water until the pasta is just covered and give everything a really good mix.
5. Cover the tray with foil, bake for 30 minutes, then remove from the oven and serve with garlic bread.

Cook: 35 Mins
Prep: 10 Mins

Salmon is delicious baked in the oven. This salmon is gorgeous, cooked with creamy butter beans, kale, tangy capers and plenty of spice.

Butter Bean Salmon

SERVES 4

- 4 tbsp vegetable oil
- 2 x 400g tins of butter beans, drained
- 150g cherry tomatoes, halved if large
- 50g capers
- 60g kale
- 1 red onion, peeled and thinly sliced
- 4 large salmon fillets (480g)
- 2 tsp salt
- 2 tsp black pepper
- 2 tsp onion granules
- 1 tsp smoked paprika
- 2 tsp garlic powder
- 1 tsp cayenne pepper
- 2 tsp brown sugar
- 2 tsp cornflour
- a good drizzle of olive oil

1. Preheat the oven to 200°C fan.
2. Put the vegetable oil into a 25 x 35cm roasting dish and add the butter beans, cherry tomatoes, capers, kale and red onion. Mix it all together.
3. Lay the salmon fillets on top, skin side up.
4. Put your salt, black pepper, onion granules, smoked paprika, garlic powder, cayenne pepper, brown sugar and cornflour into a small bowl.
5. Combine the spice mix well, then sprinkle all over the beans and fish.
6. Cover with foil and cook in the oven for 30 minutes.
7. Serve, with a drizzle of olive oil over the fish to finish.

Cook: 35 Mins
Prep: 15 Mins

There are so many ways to eat fish fingers and I am discovering and inventing new ways all the time! I love them cooked in a bake this way - fish fingers topped with creamy garlic potatoes.

Fish Finger Potato Bake

SERVES 4

1kg potatoes, diced with the skin on

50ml water, plus 2 tbsp

20 frozen fish fingers

50g butter

2 tbsp cornflour

300ml whole milk

300ml double cream

1 tsp salt

2 tsp garlic granules

2 tsp onion granules

100g Cheddar cheese

50g Parmesan cheese

To serve
baked beans

1. Start by popping the diced potatoes into a microwave-safe bowl and add the 50ml of water. Cover with clingfilm and microwave on a high heat for 8 minutes.
2. Remove the potatoes and drain away any excess moisture.
3. Lay the frozen fish fingers in the base of a 25 x 35cm roasting dish, then add the cubed potatoes.
4. Preheat the oven to 200°C fan.
5. Add the butter to the roasting dish, in small pinches all over.
6. Mix the cornflour and 2 tablespoons of water in a jug. Add the milk and cream and mix well.
7. Sprinkle the salt over the potatoes, along with the garlic granules, onion granules and Cheddar cheese. Pour in the liquid mixture from the jug and give everything a good stir.
8. Sprinkle over the Parmesan cheese and bake for 30 minutes.
9. Serve with piping hot baked beans.

Cook: 42 Mins
Prep: 15 Mins

If you love lasagne but hate the layering, this recipe is for you. All the same delicious flavour of a lasagne but without all the pots, all the washing and all the time. Just all in one.

Messy Lasagne

SERVES 4

4 tbsp vegetable oil

500g beef mince

250g lasagne sheets, broken into shards

2 x 400g tins of chopped tomatoes

1 tbsp Marmite

300ml hot water

2 tsp salt

2 tsp caster sugar

2 tsp cayenne pepper

1 tbsp onion granules

1 tbsp garlic granules

2 tsp dried oregano

2 tsp dried thyme

200g Cheddar cheese

To serve

300g sour cream

a small handful of chives

garlic bread

1. Preheat the oven to 200°C fan.
2. Put the oil into a 25 x 35cm roasting dish. Add the mince and break it up, using a spoon.
3. Add the lasagne shards.
4. Pour in the chopped tomatoes. Add the Marmite to the hot water and pour into the dish.
5. Put the salt, sugar, cayenne pepper, onion granules, garlic granules, dried oregano and dried thyme into a small bowl. Mix really well, then add to the roasting dish and give everything a really good stir.
6. Sprinkle over the cheese and bake for 30 minutes.
7. Take out of the oven, dollop over some sour cream and sprinkle with chives.
8. Serve with garlic bread.

Cook: 40 Mins

Prep: 10 Mins

Halloumi is such a delicious and versatile cheese and does not always need to be grilled. I like to eat it this way: grated on top of lots of vegetables in a spiced tomato sauce. That way you get a little bit of halloumi in every mouthful.

Halloumi Bake

SERVES 4

4 tbsp vegetable oil

500g passata

2 tbsp Worcestershire sauce

2 tbsp brown sauce

1 aubergine, cut into 1cm cubes

1 courgette, cut into 1cm cubes

1 red pepper, cut into 1cm cubes

1 x 198g tin of sweetcorn, drained

1 tsp chilli powder

2 tsp ground cumin

2 tsp onion granules

2 tsp garlic granules

1 tsp salt

1 tsp black pepper

2 tsp oregano

2 tsp cornflour

2 x 250g halloumi cheese, grated

To serve
baked potatoes

1. Preheat by preheating the oven to 200°C fan.
2. Put the oil into the base of a 25 x 35cm roasting dish, then pour in the passata, along with the Worcestershire sauce and brown sauce, and mix together.
3. Now add your cubed aubergine, courgette and red pepper, along with the sweetcorn. Mix again.
4. Put the chilli powder, ground cumin, onion granules, garlic granules, salt, black pepper, oregano and cornflour into a separate bowl. Mix well, then add to the roasting dish and make sure it's all mixed together well.
5. Sprinkle over the grated halloumi and bake for 30 minutes.
6. I love this with a huge baked potato!

Cook: 36 Mins **Prep: 25 Mins**

Roasting Dish

Everyone has their own way of making mac & cheese, and I change mine up often. This is my latest version, which you will love, made with cottage cheese for a tiny bit of sharpness and texture. It has the warmth of mustard running through it, and of course it's loaded with plenty of cheese.

Mac & Cheese

SERVES 4

- 500g macaroni pasta
- 500ml boiling water
- 2 x 300g creamy cottage cheese
- 200g Cheddar cheese, grated
- 1 tbsp English mustard
- 1 tsp salt
- 100g butter, melted
- 50g Parmesan cheese, grated

1. Put the uncooked macaroni into a 25 x 35cm roasting dish, then pour over the boiling water and set aside.
2. Preheat the oven to 200°C fan.
3. Put the cottage cheese into a blender with 150g of the Cheddar cheese, the mustard, salt and butter.
4. Pour the mixture into the roasting dish and mix really well.
5. Sprinkle over the remaining 50g of Cheddar cheese and the Parmesan, then cover with foil and bake for 30 minutes.
6. Take out and enjoy!

Cook: 35 Mins
Prep: 10 Mins

You cannot go wrong with a meatball dinner. Everyone is happy, everyone is full. Best thing is that these can be made in a roasting dish too.

Meatball Dinner

SERVES 4

5 tbsp vegetable oil

500g passata

200g green beans, thinly sliced

80g spinach, thinly sliced

2 tsp paprika

2 tsp ground cumin

2 tsp onion granules

2 tsp garlic granules

2 tsp salt

1 tsp sugar

1 tsp ground black pepper

3 tsp cornflour

500g beef mince

To serve

microwave mashed potatoes

1. Preheat the oven to 200°C fan.
2. Put the vegetable oil, passata, green beans and spinach into a 25 x 35cm roasting dish and mix well together.
3. Put the paprika, ground cumin, onion granules, garlic granules, salt, sugar, ground black pepper and cornflour into a small bowl and mix together.
4. Sprinkle the mixture over the vegetables in the roasting dish, reserving 1 tablespoon for the mince, and mix it all together.
5. Put the beef mince into a bowl with the tablespoon of reserved spices and mix with your hands.
6. Make the mixture into small meatballs and add them to the roasting dish in an even layer.
7. Bake in the oven for 30 minutes.
8. Remove from the oven and enjoy with some creamy mash.

Cook: 30 Mins

Prep: 20 Mins

Though it's a very American thing, I love meatloaf. It's simple, fuss-free and pleases everyone. This meatloaf has secret grated vegetables in it and is baked to perfection, with a delicious, sweet ketchup glaze to finish it off. So good with chips!

Meatloaf

SERVES 6

1 medium potato, peeled and roughly chopped
1 medium carrot, peeled and roughly chopped
1kg lamb mince
2 medium eggs
100g crispy fried onions
2 tsp garlic granules
2 tsp chilli flakes
1½ tsp salt
3 tbsp garam masala
2 tbsp cornflour
a small handful of fresh coriander, roughly chopped
vegetable oil
4 tbsp chilli sauce

To serve
chips

1. Put the chopped potato and carrot into a food processor and blitz until they are in small pieces.
2. Add the lamb mince, eggs, fried onions, garlic granules, chilli flakes, salt, garam masala, cornflour and coriander, and blitz again until you have a smooth mixture that is well combined.
3. Heat the oven to 220°C fan and drizzle a 25 x 35cm roasting dish with some oil. Set the roasting dish aside.
4. Grease the inside of a 900g loaf tin generously and add your mince mixture.
5. Bake for 30 minutes.
6. Take out of the oven and carefully tip the meatloaf out of its tin and into the roasting dish.
7. Smother the meatloaf entirely with chilli sauce and bake for another 10 minutes, until the sauce is bubbling.
8. Serve with chips.

Cook: 50 Mins
Prep: 25 Mins

Duck is a delicious meat that is perfect for roasting. I love cooking duck with citrus flavours, plenty of soy and lots of aromatic ingredients. This is zesty from the orange, sweet from the marmalade and salty from the soy.

Orange Peppercorn Duck Breast

SERVES 4

4 duck breasts (680g)

4 pak choi, halved lengthways

1 large orange, zest and juice

3 tbsp marmalade

100ml soy sauce

2 tsp garlic granules

2 tsp ground ginger

3 tsp cracked black peppercorns

2 nori sheets

To serve
microwave sticky rice

1. Preheat the oven to 200°C fan.
2. Cut slashes into the skin of each duck breast and put them into a 25 x 35cm roasting dish.
3. Add your pak choi to the roasting dish.
4. Make the spice marinade by putting the orange zest and juice into a bowl with the marmalade, soy sauce, garlic granules, ground ginger and cracked black peppercorns. Mix everything so it is combined well.
5. Tear up the nori sheets and add to the roasting dish.
6. Drizzle over the marinade and massage it into the duck and the pak choi. The duck breast should be skin side down, touching the base of the roasting dish.
7. Put the dish into the oven and bake for 20 minutes.
8. Take out, slice up the breast and serve with sticky rice.

Cook: 35 Mins
Prep: 10 Mins

I know risotto is meant for a pan, I know, but I promise you can also make it in a roasting dish. It will save you the arm ache and you'll still have a delicious risotto at the end. This is creamy with Parmesan, gorgeous with the crab and has a tiny kick from the cayenne.

Oven Crab Risotto

SERVES 4

100ml vegetable oil

2 medium onions, peeled and diced

½ a lemon, plus extra juice to serve

300g risotto rice

2 x 145g tins of crab, drained

1 tsp salt

2 tsp cayenne pepper

2 tsp garlic granules

150g cherry tomatoes

100g frozen peas

700ml hot water

100g Parmesan cheese, plus extra to serve

fresh parsley

To serve
green salad

1. Preheat the oven to 220°C fan.
2. Put the oil into a 25 x 35cm roasting dish and add the onions.
3. Squeeze over the half lemon, then chop up the lemon skin and add it to the dish.
4. Add the risotto rice and the drained crab.
5. Season with the salt, cayenne pepper and garlic granules, then add the cherry tomatoes and frozen peas.
6. Pour in the hot water and mix really well.
7. Sprinkle over the Parmesan cheese, then cover with foil and bake for 30 minutes.
8. Take out and serve with a sprinkling of lemon juice and fresh parsley, extra Parmesan and a fresh green salad.

Cook: 40 Mins **Prep:** 15 Mins

Roast dinners are pure comfort. But sometimes a roast dinner can be hard work, with lots of pans and even more washing up. This is an all-in-one roast: tender chicken, carrots, parsnips and leeks, all flavoured with rosemary and thyme.

Roast Chicken Dinner

SERVES 4

- 400g potatoes, diced, with skin left on
- 1 medium carrot, peeled and cut into 1cm coins
- 1 medium parsnip, peeled and cut into 1cm coins
- 1 leek, finely sliced
- 8 chicken drumsticks
- 100ml vegetable oil
- 2 tsp salt
- 2 tsp garlic granules
- 3 tsp ground black pepper
- 2 tsp dried rosemary
- 2 tsp dried thyme

To serve
- frozen Yorkshire puddings
- instant gravy

1. Preheat the oven to 220°C fan.
2. Put the potatoes into a 25 x 35cm roasting dish, and add the carrots and parsnips. Bake in the oven for 10-15 minutes. Take the vegetables out of the oven (leave the oven on) and add the leeks. Make sure everything is mixed well and in an even layer.
3. Lay the 8 chicken drumsticks on top.
4. Put the oil into a bowl and add the salt, garlic granules, black pepper, rosemary and thyme.
5. Drizzle the oil over the vegetables and chicken, then get your hands in and make sure it's spread all over everything.
6. Make sure the chicken drumsticks are on top of the veg.
7. Roast in the oven for 30 minutes, or until the chicken is cooked through.
8. In the last 5 minutes of baking, add your frozen Yorkshires and heat them through.
9. Make your gravy and you are ready to enjoy your one-dish roast dinner.

Cook: 50 Mins **Prep: 18 Mins**

Air Fryer

Salmon does not take long to cook at all, and in fact when it's overcooked it takes on the texture of tinned fish, which we do not want! When it's cooked in the air fryer with this simple Cajun spice seasoning, you get a delicious crust with a moist and delicate inside.

Cajun Spiced Salmon

SERVES 4

For the broccoli
1 large stalk of broccoli, cut into small florets (stalks included)
1 red onion, thinly sliced
1 tbsp garlic paste
2 tbsp oil
3 tbsp apple cider vinegar
1 tsp salt

For the salmon
4 salmon fillets
3 tbsp oil
3 tbsp Cajun seasoning spice
1 tsp salt
1 tsp sugar

To serve
2 x 250g packets of microwave rice
1 x 400g tin of red kidney beans
salt, to season
a handful of fresh coriander, chopped

1. Start by putting the broccoli florets into a bowl with the sliced red onion. Add the garlic paste, oil, apple cider vinegar and salt.
2. Mix together, then tip into the air fryer drawer and heat to 200°C. Cook for 10 minutes.
3. Put the salmon into a bowl with the oil, Cajun seasoning, salt and sugar. Coat really well.
4. Add to the top of the broccoli and cook for 8 minutes.
5. Heat the rice in the microwave as per the packet instructions.
6. Drain the kidney beans under a very hot tap, until the liquid runs clear and the beans are warmed through.
7. Mix the rice and the beans, season with salt and stir in the coriander.
8. Serve with the salmon and broccoli.

Cook: 25 Mins
Prep: 15 Mins

Puff pastry and the air fryer are a match made in heaven, as it's a great environment to amp up that crispy, puffy golden texture. These individual pies, with their classic cheese and onion flavour combination, are something you can likely make using bit and bobs you already have at home.

Cheese & Onion Potato Pies

SERVES 4

For the pies
- 1 x 500g block of shop-bought puff pastry, defrosted
- 400g ready-made mash
- 150g mature Cheddar, grated
- 1 tbsp onion granules
- 1 tsp garlic granules
- 1 tbsp freshly ground black pepper
- 1 tsp salt
- 1 medium egg, lightly beaten
- ½ tsp paprika

For the curry beans
- 50g salted butter
- 2 tsp whole cumin seeds
- 2 tsp chilli flakes
- 2 tsp curry powder
- 2 x 440g tin of baked beans

1. Take the block of puff pastry and cut it into 4 equal squares. Roll each square out to about ½cm thickness and set aside in the fridge.

2. Break up the ready-made mash and add the cheese to it, along with the onion granules, garlic granules, black pepper and salt. Mix together really well.

3. Lay out the pastry sheets and divide the potato mix between them. Wrap the pastry around the potato mix to make rough balls and flatten them into round-ish patties.

4. Mix the egg with the paprika and glaze each one generously.

5. Place them in the air fryer drawer and heat to 200°C. Cook for 15–20 minutes.

6. Make the curry beans by melting the butter in a pan and adding the cumin seeds, chilli flakes and curry powder. Cook for 30 seconds, then add the beans and heat through.

7. Serve the beans with the hot cheese and potato pies as soon as they come out of the air fryer.

photo overleaf

Cook: 40 Mins
Prep: 20 Mins

Cheese & Onion Potato Pies with Curry Beans

Chicken is such a great carrier of flavour, and these stuffed chicken breasts are a perfect example, filled with creamy, stretchy mozzarella and tart, pickled jalapeños, and glazed with a sweet chilli sauce. This makes a brilliant quick dinner.

Cheese-stuffed Chicken & Mash

SERVES 4

For the peppers
4 yellow peppers, each one cut into quarters
1 tsp oil
½ tsp salt
1 tsp black pepper

For the chicken
4 medium chicken breasts
3 tbsp oil
1 tsp salt
2 tsp paprika
2 tsp garlic granules
2 tsp black pepper
1 mozzarella ball, drained and sliced
pickled jalapeños
4 tbsp sweet chilli sauce

To serve
2 x 400g microwave mash
4 tbsp mayonnaise
½ tsp salt
3 tbsp crispy onions

1. Put the peppers into a bowl with the oil, salt and black pepper. Mix together, then put into the base of the air fryer drawer. Cook on 200°C for 5 minutes.
2. Take the chicken breasts and cut each one horizontally to create a pocket inside.
3. Place each chicken breast between 2 sheets of baking paper or clingfilm, and bash to flatten and even out the chicken.
4. Put the chicken into a bowl with the oil, salt, paprika, garlic granules and black pepper and mix really well.
5. Now stuff each chicken breast with sliced mozzarella and jalapeños. Use a skewer to close up each opening.
6. Place the chicken on top of the peppers and cook for 20 minutes at 200°C.
7. Take out after 20 minutes, brush the top of the chicken with sweet chilli sauce and cook for another 5 minutes.
8. Make the mash as per the packet instructions and put into a bowl. Mix in the mayo, salt and crispy onions.
9. Serve the mash with the chicken and peppers.

{ Cook: 40 Mins } { Prep: 15 Mins }

Prawns take little or no time to cook and are the perfect ingredient for your air fryer if you are looking for a super-quick recipe. These prawns are lightly spiced and coated in coconut for sweetness and crunch.

Chilli Coconut Prawns

SERVES 4

400g raw prawns
1 lime, juice and zest
4 cloves of garlic, grated
2 tbsp cornflour
1 tsp black pepper
2 tsp cayenne pepper
1 tbsp ground coriander
1 tsp curry powder
20g desiccated coconut
spray oil

To serve
2 x 250g packets of microwave rice
2 tbsp coconut oil
½ tsp salt
¼ tsp ground turmeric
a small handful of fresh coriander, chopped

1. Put the raw prawns into a bowl with the lime juice, zest and garlic. Mix, then add the cornflour, black pepper, cayenne, ground coriander, curry powder and desiccated coconut.

2. Mix well, adding 1 tablespoon of water at a time until you have a very thick batter that coats the prawns.

3. Spray the inside of the air fryer drawer with oil, and put in the prawns. Spray all over with oil and cook for 10 minutes at 200°C.

4. Meanwhile, microwave the rice as per the packet instructions and tip into a bowl.

5. Warm the coconut oil in a small pan, then add the salt and turmeric, mix well, tip into the rice and mix through. Stir in the coriander and serve with the cooked prawns.

photo overleaf

Cook: 18 Mins
Prep: 10 Mins

Chilli Coconut Prawns

Fajitas are a family favourite up and down the country, no matter the age of the people in your family. Sweet with peppers and spiced chicken, they are an absolute go-to. They are simple and easy to put together, and even better, the filling can be cooked in an air fryer. Perfect served in warm tortillas, for dinner or for a wrapped lunch ready to go.

Fajitas

SERVES 4

1 yellow pepper, thinly sliced

1 red pepper, thinly sliced

1 red onion, thinly sliced

500g boneless chicken thighs, thinly sliced

4 tbsp oil

1 tbsp cornflour

1 tbsp garlic powder

1 tbsp onion powder

1 tbsp dried oregano

2 tbsp cayenne pepper

2 tbsp ground cumin

1 tbsp salt

a small handful of fresh coriander, finely chopped

To serve

large tortilla wraps

100g mature Cheddar cheese, grated

garlic mayonnaise

Cook: 30 Mins   **Prep:** 20 Mins

1. Put the sliced yellow pepper into a large bowl with the red pepper and red onion and mix really well.

2. Add the sliced chicken thighs and the oil and mix until coated.

3. Add the cornflour, garlic powder, onion powder, oregano, cayenne pepper, ground cumin and salt, and mix really well.

4. Tip into the air fryer drawer and cook on 200°C for 10 minutes. Give everything a stir, then cook for a further 15 minutes.

5. Take out of the air fryer and sprinkle with fresh coriander. Serve with warmed tortillas, sprinkling cheese all over the filling. Drizzle with garlic mayo.

Traditionally gnocchi is boiled, but let me tell you that air frying gnocchi is a total game changer. It cooks to absolute perfection: crispy on the outside and soft in the middle. Cooked simply - with onions and chilli - and served with sriracha and coriander for extra flavour, this is a fast but satisfying meal.

Gnocchi

SERVES 2

- 450g fresh gnocchi
- 125g kale
- 1 red onion, thinly sliced
- 4 tbsp oil
- 3 tbsp chilli flakes
- 2 tbsp ground coriander
- 1 tsp salt
- 3 tbsp sriracha
- 150g Cheddar, grated
- a small handful of fresh coriander, finely chopped

1. Start by putting the gnocchi and kale into a large bowl with the red onions, oil, chilli flakes, ground coriander and salt.
2. Put into the drawer of the air fryer and cook at 200°C for 15 minutes.
3. Take the drawer out, squeeze over the sriracha and mix through, then sprinkle over the cheese and cook for another 5 minutes.
4. Serve with a sprinkling of chopped coriander.

Cook: 20 Mins Prep: 10 Mins

Cooking tofu in an air fryer is a revelation: I love the texture it creates. This dish is packed with bold flavours, particularly from the gochujang, and is hearty and filling, so it is best served with simple sticky rice and needs very little else.

Kimchi Tofu

SERVES 4

500g firm tofu, pressed dry and cut into 2 cm blocks

200g mushrooms, halved (I used chestnut)

250g pak choy, sliced

4 tbsp kimchi

1 tbsp garlic paste

3 tbsp gochujang paste

2 tbsp oil

2 tbsp soy sauce

3 tbsp honey

To serve

2 x 250g packets of microwave sticky rice

2 tbsp apple cider vinegar

sesame seeds

1. Put the tofu blocks into a large bowl with the mushrooms. Sprinkle in the pak choy and mix through.

2. Add the kimchi, garlic paste, gochujang paste, oil, soy sauce and honey, and mix so everything is evenly coated.

3. Heat your air fryer to 200°C.

4. Add everything to the air fryer and cook for 20 minutes, making sure to give everything a stir halfway through.

5. Microwave the rice as per the packet instructions. Tip out into a bowl, and mix in the vinegar and sesame seeds. Serve with the tofu and enjoy.

Cook: 32 Mins **Prep:** 15 Mins

One of the reasons I get put off making burgers indoors (and not on the barbecue) is the spitting and mess and clean-up that comes with making them. But when you cook burgers in the air fryer you just have to clean the air fryer. And that is worth it for the succulent, delicious outcome. These are simply spiced and simply gorgeous.

Mega Burgers

MAKES 4

800g lamb mince
2 medium eggs
30g breadcrumbs
1 tbsp garlic granules
2 tbsp onion granules
2 tbsp black pepper
1 tbsp salt
4 tbsp brown sauce
1 red onion, peeled and sliced into rings
4 slices of mature Cheddar cheese

To serve
4 burger buns
4 lettuce leaves
1 large tomato, thinly sliced
burger sauce

1. Put the lamb mince into a large bowl with the eggs, then get your hands in and mix until the egg is completely combined.

2. Now tip in the breadcrumbs, garlic granules, onion granules, black pepper and salt. Mix together until everything is evenly combined.

3. Divide the mince into 4 equal patties.

4. Grease the inside of the air fryer drawer and put the patties in – it's OK if they overlap a little, as they will shrink while they cook. Grease the top of the patties and cook for 10 minutes at 200°C.

5. After 10 minutes, brush the top of each patty with brown sauce, then put the onions on top of each one and cook for another 5 minutes.

6. Take the drawer out, add the cheese and cook for another 1 minute. Then remove from the air fryer and pop out on to a tray.

7. Toast the sliced buns for 3 minutes, until golden.

8. Make up your burgers with lettuce, tomato and burger sauce.

Cook: 28 Mins
Prep: 12 Mins

I'm sure purists will be shouting at this page, but there is more than one way to cook a steak! As long as it is moist and succulent, it doesn't matter how it is cooked. And in my opinion an air fryer is a great way to cook a large piece of steak, for a perfectly browned exterior with a moist, slightly pink interior. Simplicity at its absolute best.

Steak and Hash Browns

SERVES 4

1 x 500g rump steak
4 tbsp oil
1 tbsp salt
1 tbsp dried rosemary
3 red onions, peeled and cut into eighths
8 frozen hash browns
2 tbsp apple cider vinegar
1 tsp black pepper
4 eggs, fried (optional)

1. Start by heating the air fryer to 150°C.
2. Smother the steak in oil, salt and dried rosemary and rub all over.
3. Rub the onions in the oil mixture.
4. Put the steak into the air fryer tray, then put the onions on top and all around. Cook for 8 minutes.
5. Take out, flip the steak over and cook for another 8 minutes.
6. Take the onions and steak out and leave to rest while you cook the hash browns.
7. Turn up the air fryer to 220°C and cook the hash browns for 10-12 minutes.
8. Slice the steak, pour the juices from the bottom of the air fryer drawer into a bowl, and mix them with the vinegar and black pepper. If there isn't enough liquid, add some olive oil to make a drizzle.
9. Pour all over the steak and enjoy with the hash browns, and perhaps even a fried egg if you fancy it.

Cook: 30 Mins
Prep: 18 Mins

Tuna and sweetcorn is one of the most superior of sandwich fillings (in my humble opinion), but make it into a chimichanga and it is something else entirely. Chimichangas are like deep-fried wraps. Here we are air frying our wraps to result in a warm, oozy filling of tuna, sweetcorn and cheese. Top with some sour cream, cool cucumbers and tomatoes to really make a meal out of it.

Toasted Tuna Chimichangas

MAKES 4

- 2 x 125g tin of tuna in spring water, drained
- 1 x 340g tin of sweetcorn, drained
- 2 heaped tbsp mayonnaise
- 2 heaped tbsp chilli sauce
- 3 spring onions, thinly sliced
- 1 tbsp black pepper
- 150g mature Cheddar cheese, grated, plus extra for sprinkling
- 4 large tortillas
- spray oil

To serve
- 150g sour cream
- 1½ tbsp whole milk
- 1 tomato, deseeded and diced
- ¼ of a cucumber, deseeded and diced
- a small handful of fresh coriander, chopped
- salt

1. Put the drained tuna and sweetcorn into a bowl.
2. Add the mayonnaise, chilli sauce, spring onions, black pepper and cheese and mix really well.
3. Fill each tortilla equally and roll them up, sealing the edge.
4. Put them into the air fryer basket and spray with oil, then sprinkle over a little cheese and cook for 15 minutes at 160°C.
5. Loosen the sour cream with the milk. Separately mix together the tomatoes, cucumber, coriander and salt.
6. Serve the chimichangas with the sour cream on top and the chopped tomato mixture sprinkled over.

Cook: 30 Mins
Prep: 15 Mins

Tray Bakes

Cod cooks quickly, so it's the perfect variety of fish to cook in the oven on a tray. This delicious version is cooked with lightly spiced sweet potatoes, lemon, garlic and lots of other flavours, which makes for an all-round perfect dinner.

Baked Cod

SERVES 4

- 2 bay leaves (fresh or dried)
- 2 tbsp garlic paste
- 1 lemon, thinly sliced
- 2 tomatoes, each cut into eighths
- 500g sweet potatoes, peeled and cut into 1cm thick rounds
- 4 cod fillets, skin on
- 50ml vegetable oil
- 2 tsp salt
- 1 tsp ground turmeric
- 3 tsp paprika
- 1 tbsp cornflour
- a small handful of fresh coriander, finely chopped
- a small handful of fresh parsley, finely chopped

1. Preheat the oven to 200°C fan.
2. Put the bay leaves, garlic paste and sliced lemon into a 39cm baking tray.
3. Add the tomatoes and sweet potatoes, then add the cod fillets. Drizzle over the oil, making sure everything is coated.
4. Put the salt, turmeric, paprika and cornflour into a small bowl. Mix well, then add to the tray and stir to make sure everything gets coated.
5. Remove the cod from the tray and set aside.
6. Bake the vegetables in the oven for 25 minutes, then take out the tray, add the fish, skin side up, and bake for a further 10 minutes.
7. Serve sprinkled with the coriander and parsley.

Cook: 45 Mins
Prep: 20 Mins

This flatbread is made from cottage cheese, so it is packed with protein. It's a simple take on a flatbread without any kneading or waiting around. Simply topped with Cheddar cheese, tomatoes, pesto and basil, it is a total winner.

Cheese Loaded Flatbread

SERVES 6

oil, for greasing
600g creamy cottage cheese
3 medium eggs
½ tsp salt
½ tsp ground black pepper
100g Cheddar cheese, grated
6 sun-dried tomatoes, chopped
4 tbsp green pesto
fresh basil

To serve
green leafy salad

1. Start by heating the oven to 200°C fan. Line the inside of a 39cm baking tray with baking paper and grease well.
2. Put the cottage cheese into a blender with the eggs, salt and black pepper, and blend to a smooth paste.
3. Pour into the prepared tray and make sure it gets to all the edges.
4. Sprinkle over the Cheddar cheese and sun-dried tomatoes, drizzle over the pesto, and bake for 20 minutes.
5. Rip up some fresh basil and scatter it over the top, then serve in slices, with a green salad.

Cook: 30 Mins
Prep: 10 Mins

You don't have to go to a takeaway or food truck to have a shawarma. Now you can make it yourself, all on one tray – oven chips, lamb, spices, and all the toppings.

Shawarma Fries

SERVES 6

- 1kg thick-cut oven fries
- 500g lamb, thinly sliced
- 1 tbsp cornflour
- 1 tsp salt
- 1 tsp chilli powder
- 1 tsp chilli flakes
- 2 tsp ground cumin
- 2 tsp ground coriander
- 6 tbsp yoghurt
- a small handful of fresh coriander, finely chopped
- a small handful of fresh mint, finely chopped
- a pinch of salt
- 1 small red onion, finely sliced
- 3 tbsp pickled red cabbage

1. Preheat the oven to 220°C fan and pop the thick-cut oven fries on to a 39cm baking tray.
2. Put the lamb into a bowl with the cornflour, salt, chilli powder, chilli flakes, ground cumin and ground coriander. Mix everything together until really well combined.
3. Pop the mixture on to a sheet of foil, and fold into a parcel.
4. Put the tray of chips into the oven and bake for 15 minutes.
5. Then put the lamb parcel on the shelf below the chips and bake for a further 10 minutes.
6. Remove the chips and lamb from the oven. Take the lamb out of the foil and spread it all over the chips, then pop the tray back into the oven for 5 minutes.
7. Meanwhile, put the yoghurt into a small bowl with the coriander, mint and salt, and mix well.
8. Take the tray out of the oven. Drizzle the yoghurt over the chips and lamb, sprinkle over the red onion slices and pickled cabbage, and it is ready to serve.

photo overleaf

Cook: 40 Mins **Prep: 18 Mins**

Shawarma Fries

I love goat's cheese with caramelized onions, and this recipe pairs that brilliant flavour combination with flaky puff pastry, another thing that I really, really love. I hope you love this too!

Goat's Cheese & Onion Tart

SERVES 6

vegetable oil

3 medium onions, peeled and sliced into rings

1 tsp salt

1 tsp caster sugar

150g goat's cheese

1 tbsp dried thyme

1 x 320g sheet of ready-rolled puff pastry

honey, to drizzle

To serve
simple green salad

1. Preheat the oven to 200°C fan and line a 39cm baking tray with baking paper. Drizzle some oil over the paper and brush it all over in an even layer.
2. Lay the onion rings all over the paper and sprinkle all over with the salt and sugar.
3. Bake the onions for 10 minutes.
4. Take the tray out of the oven, dot all over with the goat's cheese and sprinkle over the dried thyme.
5. Place the puff pastry sheet on top and bake for another 20 minutes, until the pastry is golden.
6. Take out of the oven and leave for 10 minutes, then flip out on to a board.
7. Drizzle with honey, cut and enjoy with a simple green salad.

Cook: 40 Mins
Prep: 12 Mins

Garlic bread: the more loaded, the better! I've stacked my slices of bread with garlic butter, mayo-laced chicken, kimchi, spring onions and tons of melted cheese. Fully loaded!

Loaded Garlic Bread

SERVES 6

6 slices of bread
100g butter, melted
1 tbsp garlic granules
6 tbsp mayonnaise
8 cooked chicken slices, cut into strips
150g kimchi
3 spring onions, thinly sliced
150g Cheddar cheese
black sesame seeds

1. Preheat the oven to 200°C fan. Lay the bread slices on a 39cm baking tray lined with baking paper.
2. Mix the melted butter with the garlic granules. Brush this garlic butter all over the bread and bake in the oven for 5 minutes, until crisp and golden.
3. Put the mayonnaise, chicken strips, kimchi, spring onions and 100g of the Cheddar cheese into a bowl.
4. Spread the mayo mixture all over the bread, dividing it equally between the slices.
5. Sprinkle with more cheese and the black sesame seeds and bake until the cheese is bubbly and golden on top.

Cook: 25 Mins
Prep: 12 Mins

I love cornbread's texture: slightly gritty but still soft. So I've combined it with sausages, to come up with the corndog cake. This simple recipe packs so much flavour, with cumin seeds, jalapeños and cayenne pepper.

Corndog Cake

SERVES 6

375g plain flour
225g polenta
3 tsp cayenne pepper
2 tsp garlic granules
1 tsp salt
4 tsp baking powder
110g caster sugar
480ml whole milk
2 medium eggs, lightly beaten
110g butter, melted
6 sausages, cut into pieces with scissors
1 red pepper, thinly sliced
200g green jalapeños, drained
2 tsp cumin seeds

To serve
American mustard

1. Preheat the oven to 200°C fan, and line and grease the inside of a 39cm baking tray.

2. Put the plain flour into a bowl with the polenta, cayenne pepper, garlic granules, salt, baking powder and caster sugar, and whisk everything to combine.

3. Pour in the milk, eggs and melted butter and whisk to an even, thick batter, then pour into the prepared tray.

4. Sprinkle over the cut sausages, sliced red pepper, green jalapeños and cumin seeds.

5. Bake in the oven for 35–45 minutes, or until springy to the touch.

6. Drizzle over the mustard and it's ready to eat.

{ Cook: 55 Mins }   { Prep: 14 Mins }

If you like chicken skewers you will definitely love these. The chicken is marinated in ingredients that make it sweet, salty and fragrant, and the meat becomes deliciously sticky when grilled. Perfect for dinner or for a barbecue.

Yakitori Chicken Skewers

SERVES 6

5 tbsp vegetable oil

1 tsp salt

3 tsp ground black pepper

2 tbsp onion granules

100ml dark soy sauce

4 tbsp apple cider vinegar

100g apricot jam

1kg chicken thighs, diced

6 skewers

To serve
microwave sticky rice

1. Put the vegetable oil into a bowl, along with the salt, black pepper, onion granules, dark soy sauce, apple cider vinegar and apricot jam.
2. Add your diced chicken thighs and mix really well.
3. This can be made in advance to this point and left to marinate in the fridge, or it can be baked straight away.
4. Preheat the oven to 200°C fan and line a 39cm baking tray with baking paper.
5. Skewer the pieces of chicken so they are tightly packed. Put them on to the baking tray and bake for 20–25 minutes.
6. Remove from the oven and serve with sticky rice.

Cook: 30 Mins

Prep: 12 Mins

This is a simple and clever way of making an alternative to bacon, using frankfurters out of a packet or a jar. These are smoky from the smoked paprika and sweet from the maple. Perfect wedged in a buttered bap.

Frankfurter Bacon Sarnies

MAKES 6

10 frankfurter sausages
vegetable oil
4 tbsp maple syrup
1 tsp salt
1 tsp ground black pepper
3 tsp smoked paprika

To serve
6 floury baps
butter, to spread
crisps, on the side

1. Preheat the oven to 200°C fan and line a 39cm baking tray with baking paper.
2. Slice the franks lengthways as thin as you can possibly get them and put them on the tray.
3. Drizzle some oil all over them, then drizzle over the maple syrup.
4. Sprinkle with the salt, black pepper and smoked paprika.
5. Get your hands in and mix everything so the sausage slices are coated.
6. Bake in the oven for 15–17 minutes, until the sausages start to crisp up and darken.
7. Take out of the oven and serve in buttered baps, alongside your favourite flavour of crisps.

Cook: 22 Mins
Prep: 6 Mins

Pies don't have to be hard work, and this open-top pie is among the easiest you can make. Simple puff pastry, seasoned chicken, with sweet apricots and tons of parsley.

Open Chicken Pie

SERVES 6

2 large chicken breasts, thinly sliced

10 tbsp mayonnaise

2 tsp salt, plus a little extra

4 tsp garlic granules

4 tsp onion granules

4 tsp chilli flakes

1 tsp ground cinnamon

100g chopped apricots

a small handful of fresh parsley, finely chopped

1 x 320g sheet of ready-rolled shortcrust pastry

1 medium egg, lightly beaten

To serve

green salad

1. Preheat the oven to 200°C fan and put a 39cm baking tray on the middle shelf to heat up.

2. Put the chicken slices into a bowl with the mayonnaise. Sprinkle in the salt, garlic granules, onion granules, chilli flakes, cinnamon, chopped apricots and parsley and mix to combine. Set aside.

3. Lay the pastry on your warmed tray, then add the filling and spread it out, leaving the outer edge untouched by about 2cm.

4. Bring the outer edges inwards to encase some of that filling.

5. Brush lightly with the egg around the exposed pastry edge, sprinkle with a little salt and bake for 25 minutes.

6. Cut into squares and enjoy with a simple salad.

Cook: 35 Mins

Prep: 14 Mins

Steak can be cooked in the oven and I'm about to show you how. All you need is one tray, an oven, potatoes, steak and some excitement.

Steak & Wedges

SERVES 4

4 medium potatoes, cut into wedges
100ml vegetable oil
1 tbsp dried rosemary
1 tbsp garlic granules
1 tbsp smoked paprika
1 tsp salt, plus a little extra
1 tbsp cornflour
4 beef steaks
vegetable oil
a large pinch of ground black pepper

To serve
instant gravy

1. Preheat the oven to 200°C fan.
2. Put the potato wedges on a 39cm baking tray. Drizzle the oil evenly over them and bake for 15 minutes.
3. Put the dried rosemary, garlic granules, smoked paprika, salt and cornflour into a small bowl.
4. After 15 minutes, remove the wedges from the oven and sprinkle over the spice mix, making sure to coat all the potatoes evenly. Return the wedges to the oven for another 15 minutes.
5. Take the steaks and bash them until flat and thin. Drizzle oil all over them and sprinkle with salt and pepper on both sides.
6. Take the wedges out of the oven and dish up.
7. Pop the steak on the hot tray and bake for 5 minutes.
8. Make the gravy, and by the time the steak is ready, it will be time to eat.

Cook: 35 Mins
Prep: 10 Mins

You don't need a tandoor oven to make tandoori drumsticks. All you need are some chicken legs, ready-made tandoori paste and a few other ingredients, and before you know it you will have the most delicious tandoori chicken on your plate.

Tandoori Chicken Drums

SERVES 6

500g Greek yoghurt
100ml vegetable oil
1 lemon, juice and zest
2 tsp salt
3 tbsp garlic paste
3 tbsp ginger purée
5 tbsp tandoori masala
3 tbsp tomato paste
1 tbsp paprika
1kg chicken drumsticks

To serve
naan bread

1. Put the yoghurt, vegetable oil, lemon juice and zest into a large bowl. Add the salt, garlic paste, ginger paste, tandoori masala, tomato paste and paprika and mix really well.

2. Cut slits in your chicken drumsticks so that the flavour can penetrate, then add them to the marinade, making sure to get all the chicken evenly coated.

3. You can either do this in advance and leave the drumsticks in the fridge overnight, or you can bake them straight away.

4. Preheat your oven to 200°C fan. Line and lightly grease the inside of a 39cm baking tray.

5. Lay the drums in a line on your baking tray and bake in the oven for 35 minutes.

6. Remove from the oven and enjoy with some naan.

photo overleaf

Cook: 48 Mins
Prep: 9 Mins, plus marinating (if you want to)

Tandoori Chicken Drums

Deep Fried

These cheese balls use so few ingredients it's almost like magic! For anyone who loves cheese, I won't have to convince you. Crispy on the outside and gooey in the middle, cheese is always better deep fried, and these balls are no different. There is no going back once you've tried them.

Cheese Balls

SERVES 8

350g extra mature Cheddar cheese, grated

50g plain flour

3 medium eggs, lightly beaten

vegetable oil, for frying

To serve
hot sauce

1. Put the cheese into a large bowl. Sprinkle the flour all over the cheese, making sure it all has an even coating.

2. Add the eggs and get your hands in to form a dough.

3. Make the dough into small balls, about the size of a Brussels sprout, making sure they are tightly packed. Set aside.

4. Pour the oil into a high-sided pan to come about a third of the way up the sides, and heat it to 160°C. Have a plate ready, lined with kitchen paper.

5. Working in batches, fry the balls for 5–6 minutes, until the exterior is golden brown and crispy.

6. Serve with hot sauce.

Cook: 24 Mins
Prep: 6 Mins

I have lived a life trying to find the best chips in the land. Sometimes that search leads me straight back to my own house. No triple-frying or over-prepped potatoes here: we are simply deep-frying chipped potatoes to make the best, most delicious chips.

Chips

SERVES 4

1kg potatoes, cut into chip shapes, skin on

4 cloves of garlic, unpeeled

1 sprig of rosemary

salt, for seasoning

oil, for frying

To serve

mayonnaise

ketchup

1. Start by finding a pan that you can fit all your potatoes into at once.
2. Put the potatoes into the pan. Add the garlic and rosemary and sprinkle in about 1 heaped tablespoon of salt.
3. Pour in the oil, to come about 2cm above the potatoes.
4. Put the pan on the hob on a medium heat. Leave it there for the oil to come up to temperature. The oil will slowly cook the chips from the inside out. This can take 30 minutes.
5. Have a plate ready, lined with kitchen paper.
6. As soon as all the chips are floating, take them out with a slotted spoon and sprinkle them with salt.
7. Enjoy with mayonnaise or ketchup, or both.

Cook: 30 Mins
Prep: 10 Mins

I love frying chicken wings – nothing will give you a crispier wing than when you deep fry them. These are coated in mayo and a seasoned flour. Perfect every single time.

Chicken Wings

SERVES 6

1.5kg chicken wings, drums and flats separated
270g mayonnaise
300g plain flour
200g rice flour
2 tbsp salt
4 tbsp paprika
3 tbsp garlic granules
3 tbsp onion granules
2 tbsp dried coriander
oil, for frying

To serve
sriracha sauce

1. Put the wings on a large baking tray.
2. Add the mayonnaise, then get your hands in there and mix everything really well, so the wings are coated.
3. Put the plain flour, rice flour, salt, paprika, garlic granules, onion granules and dried coriander into a bowl. Mix thoroughly, so all the dry ingredients are combined.
4. Sprinkle the dry mix all over the wings, then get your hands in and make sure everything is coated.
5. Pour the oil into a large pan so that it comes two-thirds of the way up and heat it to 150°C. Have a large tray ready, lined with kitchen paper.
6. When the oil is hot, begin frying the wings in batches, for 6–8 minutes. Put them on the kitchen paper to drain.
7. Serve with sriracha.

Cook: 32 Mins
Prep: 9 Mins

Kebabs are always better when they are deep fried, because it's the only way you get that slightly crispier exterior. These are flavourful and hearty and work so well in a pitta, or in a wrap, but they are also delicious just as they are, served with a dip on the side.

Chicken Seaweed Kebabs

MAKES 12–15

7 nori sheets

500g chicken mince

2 tbsp cornflour

2 tsp salt

1 medium egg

2 tsp garlic paste

2 tsp ginger paste

3 tsp chilli flakes

3 tbsp sesame seeds

3 spring onions, finely sliced

a small handful of fresh coriander, finely chopped

oil, for frying and greasing

To serve

soy sauce

1. Put the nori sheets into a processor and blitz to a fine dust. Tip into a bowl and add the chicken mince, along with the cornflour, salt, egg, garlic paste, ginger paste and chilli flakes.

2. Tip out into a bowl and add the sesame seeds, spring onions and coriander. Mix to combine.

3. Pour the oil into a high-sided pan, to come about 3cm up the sides.

4. Have ready a small bowl of oil for your fingers, and a plate lined with kitchen paper for draining.

5. When the oil in the pan is heated to about 160°C, dip your fingers into the oil in the small bowl and grease your hand.

6. Take small handfuls of the chicken mix and shape them into patties. Working in batches, drop them into the oil and fry for 4 minutes on each side.

7. Put them on the kitchen paper to drain.

8. Serve with soy sauce.

Cook: 32 Mins **Prep:** 14 Mins

This is ravioli but not as you know it. Deep fried it becomes spectacular. The pasta gets really crunchy in the hot oil and is perfect as a snack to put in front of people for them just to dig in.

Crispy Ravioli Snack

SERVES 6

500g fresh ravioli
oil, for frying
salt

To serve
ketchup

1. Start by unpacking your ravioli, making sure to separate them.
2. Pour the oil into a deep pan, to come two-thirds of the way up the sides. Heat the oil to 150°C and have a plate ready, lined with kitchen paper.
3. When the oil is hot, drop in the ravioli one at a time, working in batches and making sure you don't overcrowd the pan. As always, be careful not to splash the hot oil.
4. Fry until crisp and golden.
5. Lift out with a slotted spoon on to the kitchen paper and sprinkle with salt.
6. Enjoy with ketchup.

Cook: 15 Mins
Prep: 2 Mins

When people come over, I don't really do tea and biscuits, I do tea and 'something deep fried'. That can come in many forms, but pakoras are a surefire go-to. These are sweet from the corn and crisped to perfection.

Corn Pakoras

SERVES 4

2 x 326g tins of sweetcorn, drained

1 red onion, peeled and diced

a small handful of fresh coriander, finely chopped

2 tsp chilli flakes

2 tsp cumin seeds

2 tsp coriander seeds, lightly crushed

1 tsp salt

150g chickpea flour

water

oil, for frying

For the yoghurt mint sauce

250g Greek yoghurt

3 tbsp mayonnaise

3 tsp mint sauce

2 cloves of garlic, grated

a pinch of salt

1. Start by making sure the corn is drained and any excess moisture removed.

2. Put the corn into a bowl with the onion, coriander, chilli flakes, cumin seeds, coriander seeds and salt.

3. Mix well, then add the chickpea flour – you will have a dry mixture.

4. Start adding water slowly, mixing each time, until you have a thick batter that coats the corn.

5. Mix all the ingredients for the yoghurt mint sauce in a bowl.

6. Pour about 4cm of oil into a high-sided pan. Get the pan on a medium to high heat and have a plate ready, lined with kitchen paper.

7. When the oil is at 170°C, working in batches, start adding tablespoons of the mixture to the hot oil and fry on both sides for about 3 minutes each, until crisp and golden.

8. Drain on the kitchen paper.

{ Cook: 28 Mins   { Prep: 15 Mins

I don't think I bang on enough about how much I love to fry cheese. If, like me, you love it too, then this is a recipe for you. Crispy filo with a paprika-sprinkled string cheese interior: so simple and with so few ingredients - what is not to love?

Fried Cheese

MAKES 14

14 cheese strings

1 x 270g packet of frozen filo sheets, defrosted

1 egg, lightly beaten

paprika

salt, to season

oil, for frying

To serve

tomato chutney

1. Start by unwrapping the cheese strings and setting them to one side.
2. Cut each of the 7 rectangular sheets of filo in half, so you have 14 square sheets.
3. Have the beaten egg ready in the bowl, with a pastry brush.
4. Place a square of filo in front of you, turned towards you so it looks like a diamond shape.
5. Place a stick of cheese in the centre, horizontally. Sprinkle generously with the paprika and salt.
6. Paint a line of egg wash all around all four edges of the filo, then flap over the right- and left-hand pieces of filo, so the cheese is encased. Fold over the piece closest to you and roll.
7. Brush with egg and seal.
8. Do the same with the other 13 squares.
9. Pour some oil into a high-sided frying pan, to come about one-third of the way up the sides, and heat to about 150°C.
10. Gently drop the cheese filo sticks into the oil and fry until golden brown.
11. Drain on a plate lined with kitchen paper.
12. Serve hot, with tomato chutney for dipping.

Cook: 38 Mins

Prep: 8 Mins

Fried Cheese

Deep-fried bread is insanely good and I will deep fry any type of bread without hesitation. But this is a particularly good version, made with naan pieces dipped in a spiced chickpea flour batter. You will love it.

Masala Naan

SERVES 4

400g chickpea flour, sieved

2 tsp salt

3 tsp cumin seeds

3 tsp coriander seeds, lightly crushed

1 tsp onion seeds

2 tsp chilli flakes

a small handful of fresh coriander, chopped

1 medium egg

300-350ml cold water

4 naans, chopped into chunks

oil, for frying

To serve
ketchup

1. Start by putting the sieved chickpea flour into a large bowl with the salt. Add the cumin seeds, coriander seeds, onion seeds, chilli flakes and fresh coriander and mix it all really well.

2. Add the egg and some cold water, then keep adding water and whisking until you have a thick batter.

3. Pour the oil into a high-sided pan to come about two-thirds of the way up the sides, and heat to 170°C. Have a plate ready, lined with kitchen paper.

4. Take a chunk of naan and dip it into the batter. Working in batches, drop it into the oil and fry till golden brown and puffy.

5. Serve hot, with ketchup.

Cook: 24 Mins   **Prep: 12 Mins**

Think banana bread, spiced and nutty, but deep fried, like a doughnut! Cake is great baked, but cake is even better deep fried!

Banana Cake Balls

SERVES 4

For the cake
110g unsalted butter, softened
75g caster sugar
2 small bananas, roughly mashed
2 medium eggs
100g pecans, roughly chopped
2 tsp ground cinnamon
200g self-raising flour
oil, for frying
icing sugar, for dusting

To serve
hazelnut chocolate spread

1. Start by putting the soft butter into a bowl with the sugar and mixing really well.
2. Add the bananas and eggs and mix thoroughly.
3. Now add the pecans, cinnamon and self-raising flour. Mix well and set to one side.
4. Pour the oil into a high-sided pan to come about two-thirds of the way up the sides, and heat it to 160°C. Have a plate ready, lined with kitchen paper.
5. Working in batches, drop heaped teaspoons of the batter into the oil and fry for about 5–6 minutes, until they are a deep golden brown on both sides.
6. Dust generously with icing sugar and eat with a hazelnut chocolate dip.

{ Cook: 24 Mins { Prep: 12 Mins

This is a great dessert if you want to look like you made a ton of effort and show off a bit but you don't have much time or patience. When deep fried, shop-bought cannelloni rolls are a great carrier of delicious sweet fillings. These are fried, dipped in syrup, coated in coconut and filled with an orange cream.

Sweet Crunchy Cannelloni

MAKES 20

For the cream
2 x 250g pots of mascarpone cream
10 tbsp icing sugar
2 tsp vanilla bean extract
zest of 1 orange

For the cannelloni
1 x 250g box of cannelloni
200g golden syrup
50ml water
juice of 1 orange (use the juice of the zested orange, above)
1 tsp orange blossom water
75g desiccated coconut
oil, for frying

To serve
hot cup of tea

1. Start by making the cream filling. Put the mascarpone cream into a bowl and whisk until smooth.
2. Add the icing sugar, vanilla bean extract and orange zest and whisk to combine.
3. Transfer the mixture to a piping bag and put it into the fridge.
4. Pour the oil into a high-sided frying pan, to come about two-thirds of the way up the sides, and heat to 160°C. Have a plate ready, lined with kitchen paper.
5. Fry the cannelloni for a few minutes, until fluffy and puffy and golden. Drain on the kitchen paper.
6. Put the golden syrup into a pan with the water, orange juice and orange blossom water, and heat until everything is combined.
7. Put the desiccated coconut on a plate.
8. Dip the fried cannelloni into the syrup one at a time until coated, then dip them into the coconut and set aside.
9. Once you have done them all, pipe the cream into the holes in the cannelloni and enjoy alongside a hot cup of tea.

photo overleaf

Cook: 40 Mins
Prep: 12 Mins

Sweet Crunchy Cannelloni

Cookies don't need much help, they are great as they are, until I get my hands on them, of course. These cookie dough balls are wrapped in puff pastry and deep fried. They are great to assemble ahead, but fry them at the last minute so they can be eaten hot and served with ice cream.

Warm Cookie Dough Balls

MAKES 12

100g unsalted butter, softened

125g soft brown sugar

1 tsp vanilla bean extract

85g plain flour

75g chocolate chips

1 x 320g ready-rolled puff pastry sheet

oil, for frying

icing sugar, for dusting

To serve
your favourite ice cream

1. Put the soft unsalted butter into a bowl with the soft brown sugar and mix until combined.
2. Add the vanilla bean extract and mix in.
3. Tip in the flour and chocolate chips and mix really well, until a dough is formed.
4. Divide the mixture into 12 equal balls and set aside.
5. Take the pastry and roll it out so it is a little thinner. Divide the pastry into 12 equal squares.
6. Take a dough ball and place it on a square, then wrap to encase in pastry.
7. Repeat with the rest of the pastry and dough, placing them all on a tray, and leave them in the fridge for 30 minutes or in the freezer for 15 minutes.
8. Pour the oil into a high-sided pan, to come about two-thirds of the way up the sides, and heat to 150°C. Have a tray ready, lined with kitchen paper.
9. Working in batches, fry the dough balls for about 3–6 minutes, or until a deep golden brown.
10. Dust with icing sugar and serve warm, with your favourite ice cream.

photo overleaf

Cook: 28 Mins, plus chilling

Prep: 10 Mins

Warm Cookie Dough Balls

Deep Fried / 173

Cake Tin

Upside-down cakes are not just for pineapples – oh no, they are for blueberries too! This cake is so straightforward to make. It has a simple blueberry layer in the base, which when turned out looks glorious. With a hint of thyme running through it, it tastes stunning too.

Blueberry Upside-down Cake

SERVES 8

For the berry layer
200g fresh blueberries
1 tbsp cornflour
2 tbsp caster sugar
1 tsp dried thyme

For the cake
125g unsalted butter, softened
125g caster sugar
2 medium eggs
125g self-raising flour, sieved
1 tsp vanilla extract
1 tsp almond extract

For the glaze
3 tbsp honey
1 tsp dried thyme

1. Preheat the oven to 180°C fan. Grease the inside of a 23cm cake tin and line with baking paper.

2. Put the fresh blueberries into a bowl with the cornflour, caster sugar and dried thyme. Mix together well, then tip into the base of the tin.

3. Put the unsalted butter into a mixer bowl and whip until it is light and fluffy and pale in colour. Tip in the caster sugar and whip everything until it's light, almost bright white and very fluffy.

4. Lower the speed and add 1 egg, then increase the speed to incorporate it. Do the same with the second egg.

5. Tip in your sieved flour, vanilla extract and almond extract, and fold through until you have a smooth batter.

6. Tip the batter on top of the blueberries. Level off the top and tap the tin on your work surface – a few sharp taps should remove any air bubbles.

7. Bake in the oven for 25–30 minutes, or until a skewer comes out clean.

8. Leave the cake in the tin for 10 minutes before turning out.

9. Warm the honey with the dried thyme and brush all over the cake.

Cook: 60 Mins
Prep: 12 Mins

photo overleaf

Blueberry Upside-down Cake

If making cake completely from scratch is not your thing, or perhaps if you want to start small, then this recipe is perfect for you. I've used a box cake mix but amped it right up by adding juicy tinned pineapple, coconut and lime. No one need ever know this beautiful cake started life in a box!

Box Pineapple Cake

SERVES 8

For the cake
80ml coconut oil
1 x 432g tin of pineapple in juice
2 limes, juice and zest
3 medium eggs
30g desiccated coconut
425g vanilla box cake mix

For the icing
40g desiccated coconut
200g unsalted butter
400g icing sugar, sieved
dried pineapple

To serve
yoghurt

Cook: 55 Mins, plus cooling
Prep: 8 Mins

1. Preheat the oven to 180°C fan. Grease the base and sides of two 23cm round cake tins, and line with baking paper.
2. Put the coconut oil into a blender jug, along with the tin of pineapple and all the juice. Add the lime zest and juice, eggs and coconut.
3. Add the vanilla cake mix and blend until smooth.
4. Divide the mixture between the two cake tins and bake for 25–30 minutes.
5. Take the cakes out of the oven and leave to cool in the tins for 10 minutes, then turn out and leave to cool on a rack.
6. For the icing, toast the desiccated coconut in a pan till golden. Take off the heat and leave to cool.
7. Whip the unsalted butter until light and fluffy. Then add the icing sugar and whisk until incorporated and fluffy.
8. Put one of the cakes on to a serving dish, and spread with half the buttercream.
9. Place the second cake on top and add the rest of the buttercream, then sprinkle over the toasted coconut and dried pineapple.
10. Serve in wedges, with dollops of yoghurt.

Brown butter gives an incredible depth of flavour to this cake. If you make just a little bit of extra effort by browning the butter and toasting the flour, what is otherwise a very simple cake becomes simply stunning.

Brown Butter Pecan Coffee Cake

SERVES 8

For the cake
250g unsalted butter
250g self-raising flour, sieved
250g caster sugar
4 medium eggs
1 tsp baking powder
3 tbsp instant coffee granules
3 tbsp boiling water

For the buttercream
200g pecans, finely chopped
200g unsalted butter
400g icing sugar, sieved
1 tbsp instant coffee granules
1 tbsp boiling water

1. Put the unsalted butter into a pan and let it melt, then boil until it is frothy and a deep golden brown. Take off the heat and transfer to your mixing bowl, then leave to cool for a few minutes.

2. Pop your flour into a non-stick pan and toast until it becomes a light brown colour and no longer stark white. Keep stirring – this can take a few minutes. Take off the heat and set aside to cool.

3. Preheat the oven to 180°C fan. Lightly grease the inside of two 23cm cake tins, line with baking paper, and set aside.

4. Begin whipping the butter until the mixture is lighter in colour and fluffier. Add the caster sugar and whip till the mixture is really light in colour and fluffy in texture.

5. Add the eggs one by one, making sure to incorporate them well after each addition.

6. Sieve the flour and the baking powder into the butter mixture.

7. Put the coffee granules into a cup with the boiling water, and mix. Add to the flour mixture and mix, using a spatula, until you have a light and smooth batter.

continued overleaf

Cook: 65 Mins, plus cooling
Prep: 12 Mins

8. Divide the mixture between two tins and level off the top. Bake for 25–30 minutes, until a skewer inserted comes out clean.

9. Leave to cool in the tins for 15 minutes, then turn the cakes out on to a cooling rack and leave to cool completely.

10. Now make the buttercream. Start by toasting the pecans, until they are a deep golden-brown colour. Take off the heat to cool completely.

11. Put the butter into a saucepan and let it melt until frothy and light golden brown. Pop it into a bowl and leave to cool completely – you can speed this up by popping it into the fridge or freezer for a few minutes.

12. As soon as the butter is cool, add the icing sugar.

13. Put the coffee granules into a cup with the boiling water and mix.

14. Mix the butter and icing sugar until you have a smooth mixture, then add the coffee mixture and mix well. Stir in the cooled toasted pecans.

15. Once ready to put together, place one cake on a serving plate or cake stand. Spread half the buttercream in an even layer all the way to the edges.

16. Place the second cake on top and spread with the rest of the buttercream.

17. It is ready to enjoy.

This is one of the first cakes I ever made. I don't remember where I saw the recipe, an old cookery book perhaps, or a magazine cutting, but I've wanted to recreate it for years and so I finally did. I love the apples in this cake, and the buttery, sugary crust that sits on top at the end. Totally moreish.

Butter Apple Cake

SERVES 8

For the cake

125g unsalted butter, softened

125g caster sugar

2 medium eggs

125g self-raising flour, sieved

1 tsp ground nutmeg

2 medium green apples, peeled and diced into 1cm cubes

50g caster sugar

For the butter topping

60g unsalted butter, melted

60g caster sugar

a pinch of salt

icing sugar, to dust

To serve

clotted cream

1. Preheat the oven to 180°C fan. Grease the base and sides of a 23cm cake tin and line with baking paper.

2. Put the soft butter into a mixing bowl with the caster sugar, eggs, flour and nutmeg. Mix everything on a high speed for 2 minutes, until the mixture is light and fluffy.

3. Pour the mixture into the tin and level off the top. Sprinkle on the apple cubes, sprinkle over the sugar, and bake for 25 minutes.

4. To make the butter topping, put the melted unsalted butter and caster sugar into a bowl with the salt, and mix really well.

5. After the cake has had 25 minutes in the oven, take it out, drizzle over the butter-sugar mixture and bake for a further 10–15 minutes.

6. Leave to cool in the tin for 20 minutes, then remove and leave to cool on a rack.

7. Dust with icing sugar and serve with clotted cream.

Cook: 60 Mins
Prep: 16 Mins

Flapjacks are such an easy thing to make and they're a firm favourite in our house. I have taken to making them a million different ways, and this is one of my favourites. Buttery, spiced simply, sweet with carrots and raisins, and made in a round tin and cut into wedges, it's like a carrot cake crossed with a flapjack.

Carrot Cake Flapjack

MAKES 8

For the flapjack
230g unsalted butter
160g golden syrup
160g soft brown sugar
450g porridge oats
1 medium carrot, peeled and grated
100g raisins
2 tsp mixed spice

For the frosting
75g unsalted butter, softened
75g full fat cream cheese, room temperature
150g icing sugar, sieved
1 tsp vanilla bean extract

To serve
cup of tea or coffee

Cook: 45 Mins
Prep: 14 Mins

1. Preheat the oven to 170°C fan. Lightly grease the inside of a 23cm cake tin and line with baking paper.

2. For the flapjack, put the unsalted butter, golden syrup and soft brown sugar into a small pan and heat until the sugar has dissolved and the butter has melted. Set aside.

3. Put the porridge oats into a large bowl with the grated carrot, raisins and mixed spice. Mix it well until everything is combined.

4. Pour in the liquid mixture and stir until everything is evenly coated.

5. Tip out into the prepared tin and press down firmly so the flapjack is tightly packed, then pop into the oven and bake for 20 minutes.

6. After 20 minutes, take out of the oven and press down any of the bits that have fluffed up, using the back of a spoon.

7. Leave in the tin until completely cooled. Then take out of the tin and cut into wedges.

8. To make the frosting, put the unsalted butter and cream cheese into a bowl and mix until well combined and an even colour.

9. Add the icing sugar and vanilla and mix until you have a smooth icing.

10. Ice the entire top of the flapjack, then pull out wedges and enjoy with a hot drink.

I love chai, but for me it always has to have some cake served with it, so I thought why not combine the two together? This recipe is for a simple sponge cake, aromatic with vanilla, but made extra special by the pot of chai on the side to pour all over your cake before eating.

Chai Cake

SERVES 8

For the cake
125g unsalted butter, softened
125g caster sugar
2 medium eggs
125g self-raising flour, sieved
1 tsp vanilla bean paste

For the chai
200ml whole milk
1 x 397g tin of condensed milk
410g evaporated milk
4 tea bags
6 cardamom pods, crushed
3 bay leaves
2 cinnamon sticks
2 star anise

1. Preheat the oven to 180°C fan. Grease the inside of a 23cm cake tin and line with baking paper.
2. Put the soft unsalted butter into a bowl and whisk until light and smooth. Add the caster sugar and whisk until the mixture is light and fluffy, and almost white in colour.
3. Lower the speed and add 1 egg, then increase the speed to incorporate it. Do the same with the second egg.
4. Add the self-raising flour and vanilla and fold the mixture until you have a light, fluffy and even cake batter.
5. Pour the batter into the tin and level the top. Bake for 25–30 minutes, until a skewer inserted comes out clean.
6. Meanwhile, make the chai by putting the whole milk into a pan with the condensed milk, evaporated milk, tea bags, cardamom pods, bay leaves, cinnamon sticks and star anise.
7. Mix it all together, then put it on a medium heat and bring to the boil, stirring. As soon as it comes to the boil, leave it to simmer for 10 minutes, then take off the heat.
8. Take the cake out of the oven and leave it in the tin for 10 minutes. Then turn out the cake and cut into wedges.
9. Take the chai off the heat as soon as it comes to the boil, then strain through a sieve into a jug.
10. Serve each slice of cake with the hot chai poured over it to soak in.

Cook: 60 Mins
Prep: 9 Mins

These cinnamon scrolls are like scones but rolled. See what I did there? The texture should be short and crumbly. They are absolutely delicious on their own, just as they are, rolled in cinnamon and drizzled with icing – perfect with a cup of tea.

Cinnamon Scrolls

MAKES 12

For the cinnamon paste
60g unsalted butter, very soft
1 tsp ground cinnamon
35g caster sugar

For the dough
500g self-raising flour, plus extra for rolling out
150g cold unsalted butter, diced
2 tsp baking powder
2 tsp caster sugar
1 tsp vanilla extract
3 medium eggs, lightly beaten
60ml whole milk

For the icing
150g icing sugar, sieved
6 tsp cold water
1 tsp vanilla extract
a pinch of ground cinnamon

To serve
cup of tea

1. Start by making the cinnamon paste. Put the soft unsalted butter into a small bowl with the cinnamon and caster sugar. Mix together until you have a smooth, even paste. Set aside.

2. Preheat the oven to 200°C fan. Grease the inside of two 23cm cake tins and line with baking paper.

3. Put the self-raising flour into a large bowl and add the cold butter. Get your hands in and rub the butter into the flour until there are no large lumps and the butter is incorporated.

4. Add the baking powder and caster sugar, mix together and make a well in the centre.

5. Add the vanilla to the lightly beaten eggs and then pour in the whole milk. Mix everything together and pour into the dry mixture.

6. Use a palette knife to bring the dough together as much as you can. Then get your hands in and bring the dough together without kneading.

7. Tip out on to a lightly floured surface and roll out to an even rectangle of 25 x 35cm, making sure the longest side is closest to you.

8. Spread the cinnamon paste mixture all over the pastry, then roll it up from the longest side, so you have a long sausage shape, and cut it into 12 equal pieces.

Cook: 48 Mins
Prep: 14 Mins

continued overleaf

9. Place 6 scrolls in one prepared tin and 6 in another. Pop them into the oven for 15–18 minutes.

10. Mix the icing sugar, water and vanilla together to make an icing.

11. Once the scrolls are out of the oven and have cooled down, drizzle the icing all over, sprinkle on the ground cinnamon and leave in the tin for 15 minutes before taking out and enjoying with a nice cup of tea.

This is like a bread-and-butter pudding but - simply put - better. It's made with an easy vanilla custard, which is baked around chunks of buttery croissant, laced with raspberries and white chocolate. It's comforting, warm and really hits the spot.

Croissant Berry Pudding Slices

SERVES 8

4 large croissants
3 medium eggs
300ml double cream
100ml whole milk
1 tsp vanilla extract
3 tbsp caster sugar
100g fresh raspberries
50g white chocolate, chopped
icing sugar, to dust

To serve
clotted cream

1. Preheat the oven to 160°C fan. Grease the inside of a 23cm cake tin.

2. Take a sheet of baking paper, large enough to cover the base and sides of the tin, scrunch it into a ball, then un-scrunch the paper, flatten it out, and fit it into the tin. Grease the inside of the paper.

3. Rip the croissants into small shreds and put them into the tin.

4. Put the eggs into a bowl and whisk until broken up. Add the double cream, whole milk, vanilla and caster sugar, and mix until really well combined.

5. Get a sieve, and strain the custard mix through the sieve, straight on to the croissants.

6. Put the fresh raspberries on top, sprinkle over the white chocolate, and bake for 35 minutes.

7. Remove from the oven and leave to cool, then chill in the fridge. Dust with icing sugar and serve cut into wedges, with clotted cream.

photo overleaf

Cook: 45 Mins
Prep: 8 Mins

Croissant Berry Pudding Slices

This is like a baked cheesecake but easier. There is no pressure for straight lines or perfect bakes. It is delicious and simple, with a crushed Biscoff biscuit base, a cottage cheese filling and a fruity topping. No fuss, no frills, just flavour.

Cottage Cheesecake

SERVES 8

130g Biscoff biscuits
600g cottage cheese
2 medium eggs
4 tbsp caster sugar
2 tbsp plain flour
1 lemon, zest and juice
200g strawberry jam

To serve
pouring cream

1. Preheat the oven to 160°C fan. Grease the inside of a 23cm cake tin and line it with baking paper.
2. Break the Biscoff biscuits into the base of the tin, making sure they are in an even layer.
3. Put your cottage cheese, eggs, caster sugar, flour and lemon zest into a blender, and blend to a smooth paste.
4. Pour over the biscuit base and tap the tin on the work surface so you have an even layer.
5. Bake for 35–40 minutes, then remove from the oven and leave to cool. When cooled, chill for 4 hours or overnight.
6. To make the topping, put the jam into a pan with the lemon juice. Heat and stir until everything is warm and loose.
7. Add the jam to the chilled cheesecake and serve in wedges, not forgetting some pouring cream.

Cook: 50 Mins, plus chilling
Prep: 5 Mins

I love peanuts in all their forms. But have you ever tried frying them? Well, when fried, peanuts go to another level of flavour. This tart uses a pre-made shell which is filled with a buttery, brown sugary, cinnamony delight. If you love peanuts like I do, you are going to adore this one.

Fried Peanut Pie

SERVES 8

For the pastry
1 x 195g ready-made pastry case

For the filling
vegetable oil
125g unsalted peanuts
25g butter, melted
85g soft light brown sugar
2 medium eggs
100ml golden syrup
1 tsp vanilla extract
1½ tsp ground cinnamon
a large pinch of salt

To serve
mascarpone cream

1. Preheat the oven to 160°C fan. Take the pastry case out of its packaging and place on a baking tray. Get a plate and double line with kitchen paper.

2. Pour a 2cm layer of oil into your frying pan. Put the pan on the hob and heat on a medium heat.

3. Gently drop in the peanuts and fry until golden brown. Take out with a slotted spoon and leave to cool and drain on the kitchen paper.

4. Put the melted butter, brown sugar and eggs into a bowl and mix everything really well.

5. Now pour in the golden syrup, vanilla extract, ground cinnamon and a pinch of salt. Add the fried peanuts. Mix well, then put the mixture into the pastry case and bake for 35–40 minutes.

6. Remove from the oven and leave to cool completely, then slice into wedges and serve with mascarpone cream.

Cook: 48 Mins
Prep: 8 Mins

What I love about this cake is that you don't actually have to weigh anything with scales, you measure everything using the yoghurt pot. So this cake can be made by anyone. It is tender and moist, and can be jazzed up in so many ways - you only have to use your imagination.

Two Pots of Yoghurt Cake

SERVES 6

For the cake
2 x 110g pots of yoghurt (any kind you like)
1 pot of vegetable oil (measure with an empty yoghurt pot)
1 pot of caster sugar (measure as above)
3 medium eggs
4 pots of self-raising flour (measure as above)
1 tsp vanilla extract
½ tsp baking powder

For the icing
1 x 110g pot of yoghurt
300g icing sugar

To serve
thick double cream
strawberries

1. Preheat the oven to 180°C fan. Grease the inside of a 23cm cake tin and line with baking paper.
2. Decant the two pots of yoghurt into a bowl.
3. Fill one empty pot with oil and add that to the bowl. Fill the same pot with sugar and add to the bowl.
4. Crack the eggs into the bowl.
5. Now measure the flour, using the yoghurt pot, and add to the bowl.
6. Get the vanilla extract and baking powder in.
7. Whisk until everything is really well combined. Pour into the prepared tin and bake for 25-30 minutes.
8. Remove from the oven and leave to cool in the tin for 10 minutes, then turn out and cool completely on a rack.
9. Mix the yoghurt in a bowl with the icing sugar, and spread it on top of the cooled cake.
10. Serve with thick cream and fresh strawberries.

Cook: 40 Mins
Prep: 8 Mins

chocolate

Everyone needs to know how to make a brownie. Not only because they are top tier in the world of baked goods, but because they are brilliant for making ahead. These are great frozen and eaten on demand; you can't get quicker than that.

Chocolate Brownies

MAKES 16 SQUARES

For the brownie
18 (sticks) Twix bars
250g dark chocolate, chopped
250g unsalted butter
4 medium eggs
280g caster sugar
130g plain flour, sieved
20g cocoa powder, sieved
a pinch of salt
2 tbsp boiling water
2 tbsp instant coffee
100g roasted hazelnuts

For the ganache
300g dark chocolate, chopped
300ml double cream
50g white chocolate, chopped
a pinch of salt

To serve
ice cream

1. Start by lining the inside, base and sides of a 23cm square tin with baking paper. If you want a super fudgy brownie, I would make these ahead of time.
2. Arrange the Twix bars across the base of the tin, cutting, breaking and arranging where you need to.
3. Preheat the oven to 180°C fan.
4. For the brownie mix, put the dark chocolate into a pan with the unsalted butter and melt until smooth and runny. Set aside to cool down a little.
5. Put the eggs into a large bowl with the sugar and whisk until the mixture is really light and fluffy and pale. Pour in the liquid chocolate mixture and whisk until you have an even mixture with no streaks.
6. Add the flour, cocoa powder and salt.
7. Mix the boiling water in a cup with the instant coffee, and pour into the large bowl.
8. Mix the batter until it is smooth and glossy.
9. Stir in the roasted hazelnuts and pour the batter over the layer of biscuits. Tap the tin a few times on the worktop to make sure the batter gets in between all the gaps in the biscuits.

continued overleaf

Cook: 45 Mins, plus chilling
Prep: 22 Mins

10. Bake for 23 minutes, then take out and leave to cool completely in the tin. Once cooled, chill in the fridge for at least 4 hours or overnight.

11. To make the ganache, put the dark chocolate into a bowl. Bring the double cream to the boil in a pan and as soon as it just starts to bubble up, take off the heat and pour over the chocolate. Let it sit for a few minutes, then stir to combine.

12. Pour the mixture over the chilled brownie. Let it cool, then sprinkle over the white chocolate and a pinch of salt and leave to set in the fridge for another hour.

13. Cut into squares and enjoy with ice cream.

Chocolate mousse does not have to be tricky to make, and with this recipe it absolutely is not. Two ingredients: water and chocolate – that's it! – to make the most delicious mousse, and then a few more optional ingredients to sprinkle and serve.

Two-ingredient Chocolate Mousse

SERVES 4

265g dark chocolate
250ml fridge-cold water

To serve
100g chopped roasted hazelnuts
fresh cream
fresh berries

1. Start by melting the chocolate in the microwave, until liquid.
2. Put the 250ml of fridge-cold water into a blender jug. Pour in the melted chocolate and whip until you have a mixture that has quadrupled in size and is foamy.
3. Pour into individual pots and leave to set overnight, or for at least 4 hours.
4. To serve, sprinkle over some roasted hazelnuts and serve with berries and cream, if you like.

{ Cook: 28 Mins plus 4 hours chilling, or overnight   { Prep: 3 Mins

Much as I love buying snacks, I love making them even more. In my opinion, cereal makes a great basis for a snack, a use for it which is not considered enough. These delicious, chocolatey, wheaty snacks are highly addictive, and will have you going back for more.

Choco Chow

SERVES 4–6

230g Shreddies
50g tahini
100g unsalted butter
a pinch of salt
100g icing sugar
25g cocoa powder

1. Put the Shreddies into a large bowl.
2. Put the tahini, unsalted butter and a pinch of salt into a pan and heat until the butter has melted and the tahini has mixed with the butter.
3. Pour the mixture all over the cereal and mix well so it is all soaked in.
4. Put the icing sugar and cocoa powder into a large zip-lock bag and shake to combine.
5. Add the cereal to the bag and seal, then shake the bag around and encourage the cereal to be coated with the sweet cocoa mixture.
6. It is ready to eat straight away.

Cook: 8 Mins
Prep: 4 Mins

If you love chocolate, you will adore this cheesecake. There is chocolate in every part of it: chocolate biscuits in the base, cocoa and chocolate chips in the filling and even more chocolate on top. Chocolate on the brain!

Chocolate Cheesecake

SERVES 8

For the base
350g Oreo biscuits
175 unsalted butter, melted
a pinch of salt

For the cheesecake
900g full fat cream cheese
100g icing sugar
300ml double cream
50g cocoa powder
3 tbsp hot milk
2 tsp vanilla bean paste
100g milk chocolate chips, chopped

For the topping
200g milk chocolate, chopped
150ml boiling water
100g white chocolate, chopped

To serve
pouring cream

1. Start by lining the base and sides of your cake tin with baking paper and lightly greasing (I used a 23cm springform tin), leaving a little extra paper overhanging to help you remove the cheesecake from the tin. Set aside.

2. Put the Oreo biscuits into a food processor and blitz to a fine crumb. Add the melted butter and salt, and whizz until it comes together.

3. Tip the mixture into the base of the tin, then, using the back of a spoon, press down and pack tightly. Pop the tin into the fridge.

4. Put the cream cheese into a bowl and whisk until smooth. Add the icing sugar and double cream and whisk until combined.

5. Put half the cream cheese mixture into another bowl.

6. Put the cocoa powder and hot milk into a small cup and mix together.

7. Add the cocoa mixture to one half of the cream cheese mixture and mix really well. Set aside.

8. To the other half, add the vanilla bean paste and chocolate chips and mix through.

continued overleaf

Cook: 45 Mins, plus chilling overnight
Prep: 12 Mins

9. Dollop alternate spoonfuls of the two mixtures into the tin, until you have no more mixture left. Give the tin a sharp tap to remove any air bubbles. Level off the top and leave to chill for 4 hours, or ideally overnight.

10. To make the topping, put the milk chocolate into a bowl and pour in the boiling water. Whisk until you have a smooth mixture, then leave to cool for a few minutes.

11. Pour the chocolate topping all over the cheesecake, sprinkle with the white chocolate and pop into the freezer for 30 minutes to set.

12. Take out of the tin and serve with pouring cream.

These are scones reimagined with chocolate. With cocoa and chunks of chocolate in the dough, combined with nuttiness from the pistachios, they are perfect if you want to make something comfortably familiar but with a delicious difference.

Chocolate Pista Scones

MAKES 9

330g self-raising flour, sieved, plus extra for rolling out
20g cocoa powder, sieved
1 tsp baking powder
85g unsalted butter, cubed
4 tbsp caster sugar
50g pistachios, chopped
50g milk chocolate, chopped
150g Greek yoghurt
4 tbsp whole milk
1 tsp vanilla extract
1 tsp almond extract
1 egg, lightly beaten, to glaze

To serve
pistachio cream (available in supermarkets)

1. Preheat the oven to 200°C fan. Line and lightly grease a baking tray.
2. Put the flour, cocoa and baking powder into a bowl and mix really well.
3. Add the butter and rub it in, using your fingertips, until you have no more large lumps of butter.
4. Add the caster sugar, pistachios and milk chocolate, mix through really well, then make a well in the centre.
5. Add the yoghurt, whole milk, vanilla and almond extracts to the well, using a knife to bring it all together until no more bits of yoghurt are visible.
6. Now get your hands in and gently bring the dough together. Do not be tempted to knead, as this will result in a chewy dough. We want a dough that is crumbly and soft.
7. Lightly flour the surface of your worktop and tip the dough out on to the surface. Roll out to a 23cm square.
8. Cut into 9 squares and pop them on to the prepared tray.
9. Glaze the tops with the beaten egg and bake for 12–14 minutes.
10. Take out of the oven and leave for 5 minutes before enjoying with pistachio cream.

{ Cook: 30 Mins   { Prep: 18 Mins

I used to make this a lot when my kids were small, as it can be prepared very quickly and is easy to make ahead. I love how rich and creamy it is. Olive oil is the secret ingredient that really makes the pudding shine.

Chocolate Pudding

SERVES 6-8

400ml whole milk
300ml double cream
1 tsp vanilla bean paste
4 medium egg yolks
30g caster sugar
2 tsp cornflour
200g dark chocolate, roughly chopped
100ml olive oil
210g salted caramel
a pinch of salt

To serve
biscuits

1. Put the whole milk and double cream into a pan and stir. Heat until the mixture just comes to the boil, and as soon as it does, turn the heat right off.
2. Put the vanilla bean paste, egg yolks, caster sugar and cornflour into a medium bowl and whisk until combined.
3. Pour the hot milk on top of the egg mixture and whisk until everything is well combined.
4. Add the dark chocolate to the hot mixture and whisk to combine. Pour back into the pan and heat over a medium heat until just below boiling, stirring continuously.
5. Whisk in the olive oil.
6. I like to make this in one big dish, but you can use individual dishes too. Chill in the fridge until set.
7. Warm the salted caramel in the microwave until runny, then take the set pudding out of the fridge and spread all over. Sprinkle over the salt.
8. Serve with your favourite biscuits.

Cook: 25 Mins, plus chilling
Prep: 10 Mins

This is a great make-ahead recipe that you can pop into a jar or tin and keep for the rest of the week. The shards can be eaten in so many different ways: with ice cream, as a decoration on a cake, or simply as a snack. But best of all, you get to customize them with whatever toppings you like, making them different each and every time.

Chocolate Shards

MAKES 1 LARGE SHEET

- 2 x 100g blocks of dark chocolate
- 2 x 100g blocks of milk chocolate
- 2 x 100g blocks of white chocolate
- 100g salted pretzels
- 100g dried cherries
- 50g hazelnuts
- 1 x small packet of salted crisps

1. Start by finding a baking tray, one with sides, that will fit all 6 of the blocks of chocolate when laid out on the tray.
2. Line the tray with baking paper and preheat the oven to 100°C fan.
3. Unwrap the blocks of chocolate and lay them on the tray in whatever order you like. Pop the tray into the oven and leave for just long enough for the chocolate to melt.
4. As soon as the chocolate looks glossy, take it out and use a skewer to create some feathering as you run it through the chocolate.
5. Sprinkle on the salted pretzels, dried cherries and hazelnuts.
6. Crush the salted crisps and sprinkle them on top.
7. Leave to set in the fridge until the chocolate is hard, then break into shards and enjoy.

Cook: 12 Mins, plus chilling

Prep: 5 Mins

These were inspired by the chocolate twists you can buy at the big coffee chains. Light puff pastry, packed with an almond filling, sprinkled with chocolate chunks and baked to crispy, puffy perfection.

Chocolate Twists

MAKES 12

- 150g unsalted butter, softened
- 150g caster sugar
- 2 medium eggs
- 150g ground almonds
- 2 tsp almond extract
- 3 tbsp custard powder
- 2 x 320g ready-rolled puff pastry sheets, defrosted
- 100g dark chocolate chips
- 1 egg, lightly beaten, for glazing
- Icing sugar, for dusting

1. Line two baking trays with baking paper.
2. Put the unsalted butter and caster sugar into a bowl and beat until combined.
3. Add the eggs and mix well.
4. Now add the ground almonds, almond extract and custard powder, and combine well.
5. Lay the first puff pastry sheet on your work surface. Spread half the almond mixture over one half of the pastry, then sprinkle over half the chocolate chips.
6. Fold the other half of the pastry over the almond and chocolate, and press down lightly.
7. Cut widthways into 6 strips.
8. Do the same with the second pastry sheet.
9. Brush all the strips with egg, generously.
10. Twist the pastries twice and place them on the baking trays, pressing the ends down so they don't uncurl. Chill in the freezer for 20 minutes.
11. Preheat the oven to 200°C fan.
12. Bake for 20 minutes, until golden brown.
13. Take out of the oven and leave to cool on the tray, then dust with icing sugar and enjoy with coffee.

Cook: 45 Mins, plus chilling

Prep: 10 Mins

Everyone needs to know how to make an ace cookie. These are chocolatey, with a mallow filling and a crispy exterior. Perfect for right now or to pop unbaked into the freezer, ready to take out and bake as and when you want them. Fresh cookies on hand, all the time.

Crunchy Chocolate Chip Cookies

MAKES 12

150g unsalted butter, softened
125g soft brown sugar
100g caster sugar
1 tsp almond extract
1 medium egg
1 egg yolk
300g plain flour
½ tsp baking powder
½ tsp salt
100g milk chocolate, finely chopped
12 medium marshmallows
50g Rice Krispies
icing sugar, for dusting (optional)

To serve
cold milk

1. Preheat the oven to 150°C fan and line two baking trays with baking paper.
2. Put the soft unsalted butter into a bowl with the soft brown sugar and caster sugar, and whisk until light and fluffy.
3. Add the almond extract, whole egg and egg yolk, and mix everything to a smooth paste.
4. Drop in the plain flour, baking powder, salt and chopped chocolate and mix until a dough forms.
5. Divide the mixture into 12 equal balls.
6. Take a ball of dough, flatten it, then put a marshmallow in the centre and roll back into a ball, encasing the marshmallow completely.
7. When all 12 are done, roll each ball in the cereal until they are fully coated.
8. Pop 6 balls on each tray and bake for 15 minutes.
9. Take out of the oven and leave on the tray to cool completely.
10. Dust with icing sugar, if you like, and enjoy with a glass of cold milk.

Cook: 45 Mins
Prep: 10 Mins

Yes, I know it's easy to make a mug of hot chocolate using a shop-bought packet or jar. Believe me, I have nothing against that, but it's really lovely to enjoy an indulgent home-made hot chocolate from time to time. This is rich and thick enough to dip sweet treats in.

Hot Chocolate

MAKES 12

2 tbsp cornflour
200g dark chocolate, chopped
4 tbsp brown sugar
a pinch of salt
400ml whole milk
400ml coconut milk

To serve
whipped cream
cocoa, for dusting
biscuits

1. Put the cornflour into a bowl with the chocolate, sugar and salt. Mix it all together really well and set aside.
2. Put the milk and coconut milk into a pan and bring to the boil, then reduce the heat and add the chocolate mix. Whisk until the chocolate is mixed in and the whole thing has thickened.
3. Take off the heat, pour into mugs, and add a dollop of cream and a dusting of cocoa.
4. Serve with biscuits.

Cook: 12 Mins
Prep: 8 Mins

Thanks

Thank you firstly to the reader and buyer of this book; if you made it all the way back here, to the very last pages, you truly are one of a kind.

For the design of this book, thank you, Sarah Fraser, for always coming up with something fresh and unique. Your style changes with me and my ever-changing folds and flow of my hijab.

For the photography, thank you, Chris Terry, for capturing the food in its most authentic and natural light.

Thank you, Rob and Hollie, for the beautiful food preparation and the good vibes, always.

Thank you, Roya, for putting it all together, with such quiet and beautiful finesse, you are a wonder.

Thank you to Martha and Heather, for getting me dressed and made up to feel and look 'nearly' as good as the food. The food always wins!

Thank you to the entire team at Michael Joseph, including Ione Walder, Sukhmani Bhakar, Beatrix McIntyre, Liz Smith, Gaby Young and Louise Moore. No book is made without the team and you are all so valued and appreciated for the work you put in to get the book on the shelves.

Nadiya x

Index

A
almonds, ground: chocolate twists **225**
apples: butter apple cake **187**
apricot jam: yakitori chicken skewers **135**
apricots: open chicken pie **139**
aubergines: halloumi bake **81**

B
baby corn: beef ginger stir-fry **40**
baked beans: cheese & onion potato pie with curry beans **99**
bananas: banana cake balls **164**
beans: butter bean salmon **77**
    Cajun spiced salmon **96**
    cheese & onion potato pie with curry beans **99**
beansprouts: honey chicken udon **58**
beef: beef ginger stir-fry **40**
    keema rice **27**
    meatball dinner **85**
    messy lasagne **79**
    steak & wedges **140**
    steak and hash browns **116**
    steak and mushroom **71**
biscuits: cottage cheesecake **200**
blueberries: blueberry upside-down cake **176**
bread: cheese loaded flatbread **124**
    frankfurter bacon sarnies **136**
    loaded garlic bread **131**
    masala naan **163**
    prawn toasties **65**
broccoli: beef ginger stir-fry **40**
    Cajun spiced salmon **96**
brown butter pecan coffee cake **182-4**
brown sauce: crunchy noodle potato salad **53**
    halloumi bake **81**
    mega burgers **115**
burgers: mega burgers **115**
butter apple cake **187**
butter bean salmon **77**

C
cabbage: cabbage tuna pancake **43**
Cajun spiced salmon **96**
cakes and bakes: blueberry upside-down cake **176**
    box pineapple cake **181**
    brown butter pecan coffee cake **182**
    butter apple cake **187**
    carrot cake flapjack **188**
    chai cake **191**
    chocolate brownies **208-10**
    cinnamon scrolls **192-4**
    cottage cheesecake **200**

croissant berry pudding slices **197**

two pots of yoghurt cake **204**

cannelloni, sweet crunchy **167**

capers: butter bean salmon **77**

caramel: chocolate pudding **221**

carrots: carrot cake flapjack **188**

    meatloaf **86**

    roast chicken dinner **93**

cashews: fish & coconut curry **24**

celery: Creole style prawns **23**

chai cake **191**

cheese: air-fried gnocchi **111**

    baked feta pasta **74**

    cheese & onion potato pie with curry beans **99**

    cheese and pickle snack **42**

    cheese balls **149**

    cheese loaded flatbread **124**

    cheese-stuffed chicken & mash **102**

    fajitas **108**

    filo feta squares **57**

    fish finger potato bake **78**

    fried cheese **159**

    goat's cheese & onion tart **128**

    halloumi bake **81**

    loaded garlic bread **131**

    mac & cheese **82**

    mega burgers **115**

    messy lasagne **79**

    oven crab risotto **90**

    pan-fried gnocchi **61**

    toasted tuna chimichangas **119**

cheesecake: chocolate cheesecake **215-17**

    cottage cheesecake **200**

cherries: chocolate shards **222**

chicken: cheese-stuffed chicken & mash **102**

    chicken half-moons **47**

    chicken rice **20**

    chicken seaweed kebabs **153**

    chicken wings **151**

    fajitas **108**

    honey chicken udon **58**

    loaded garlic bread **131**

    open chicken pie **139**

    roast chicken dinner **93**

    soba chicken noodles **16**

    tandoori chicken drums **143**

    yakitori chicken skewers **135**

chilli sauce: cheese-stuffed chicken & mash **102**

    meatloaf **86**

    pan-fried gnocchi **61**

    toasted tuna chimichangas **119**

chimichangas, toasted tuna **119**

chips: homemade method **150**

    shawarma fries **125**

chocolate: choco chow **213**

    chocolate brownies **208-10**

    chocolate cheesecake **215-17**

    chocolate pista scones **218**

    chocolate pudding **221**

    chocolate shards **222**

chocolate twists **225**
croissant berry pudding slices **197**
crunchy chocolate chip cookies **226**
hot chocolate **228**
two-ingredient chocolate mousse **212**
warm cookie dough balls **170**
cinnamon scrolls **192–4**
clementines: soba chicken noodles **16**
coconut, desiccated: box pineapple cake **181**
   chilli coconut prawns **105**
   sweet crunchy cannelloni **167**
coconut milk: fish & coconut curry **24**
   hot chocolate **228**
coconut oil: box pineapple cake **181**
cod: baked cod **122**
   fish & coconut curry **24**
coffee: brown butter pecan coffee cake **182–4**
   chocolate brownies **208–10**
condensed milk: chai cake **191**
cookie dough balls, warm **170**
cookies, crunchy chocolate chip **226**
corn pakoras **157**
corndog cake **132**
cottage cheese: cheese loaded flatbread **124**
   cottage cheesecake **200**
   mac & cheese **82**
courgettes: halloumi bake **81**
crab: oven crab risotto **90**
crab stick fried rice **50**

cream: chocolate brownies **208–10**
   chocolate pudding **221**
   croissant berry pudding slices **197**
   fish finger potato bake **78**
   rice pudding **34**
   steak and mushroom **71**
cream cheese: carrot cake flapjack **188**
Creole-style prawns **23**
crisps: chocolate shards **222**
croissant berry pudding slices **197**
crumpets: savoury crumpets **66**
cucumber: dumpling salad **54**
curry: fish & coconut curry **24**
   garlicky onion & yoghurt curry **28**
   keema rice **27**
   masala meatballs **19**
   simple dhal **15**
custard powder: chocolate twists **225**

D

dhal, simple **15**
drinks: hot chocolate **228**
duck: orange peppercorn duck breast **89**
dumpling salad **54**
dumplings, golden syrup **35**

E

eggs: box pineapple cake **181**
   cabbage tuna pancake **43**
   cheese balls **149**
   cheese loaded flatbread **124**
   corndog cake **132**

crab stick fried rice **50**

croissant berry pudding slices **197**

meatloaf **86**

savoury crumpets **66**

evaporated milk: chai cake **191**

F

fajitas **108**

feta: baked feta pasta **74**

filo feta squares **57**

filo feta squares **57**

fish: baked cod **122**

butter bean salmon **77**

cabbage tuna pancake **43**

Cajun spiced salmon **96**

fish & coconut curry **24**

fish finger potato bake **78**

toasted tuna chimichangas **119**

frankfurter bacon sarnies **136**

G

garlic bread, loaded **131**

ginger: beef ginger stir-fry **40**

gnocchi: air-fried gnocchi **111**

pan-fried gnocchi **61**

goat's cheese & onion tart **128**

gochujang paste: kimchi tofu **112**

rice paper tteokbokki **31**

golden syrup: carrot cake flapjack **188**

fried peanut pie **203**

golden syrup dumplings **35**

sweet crunchy cannelloni **167**

green beans: beef ginger stir-fry **40**

meatball dinner **85**

gyoza: dumpling salad **54**

H

halloumi bake **81**

hash browns: crunchy noodle potato salad **53**

steak and hash browns **116**

hazelnuts: chocolate brownies **208–10**

chocolate shards **222**

two-ingredient chocolate mousse **212**

honey: beef ginger stir-fry **40**

blueberry upside-down cake **176**

dumpling salad **54**

filo feta squares **57**

goat's cheese & onion tart **128**

honey chicken udon **58**

kimchi tofu **112**

J

jalapeños: cheese-stuffed chicken & mash **102**

corndog cake **132**

K

kale: air-fried gnocchi **111**

butter bean salmon **77**

keema rice **27**

kidney beans: Cajun spiced salmon **96**

kimchi: kimchi tofu **112**

loaded garlic bread **131**

Index / 235

L

lamb: masala meatballs **19**
   meatloaf **86**
   mega burgers **115**
   shawarma fries **125**
lasagne, messy **79**
leeks: roast chicken dinner **93**
lemons: baked cod **122**
   cottage cheesecake **200**
   crunchy noodle potato salad **53**
   oven crab risotto **90**
   tandoori chicken drums **143**
lentils: simple dhal **15**
limes: box pineapple cake **181**
   chilli coconut prawns **105**
   honey chicken udon **58**

M

mac & cheese **82**
mangetout: fish & coconut curry **24**
maple syrup: frankfurter bacon sarnies **136**
marmalade: orange peppercorn duck breast **89**
Marmite: chicken rice **20**
   messy lasagne **79**
marshmallows: crunchy chocolate chip cookies **226**
masala meatballs **19**
masala naan **163**
mascarpone: sweet crunchy cannelloni **167**
mayonnaise: cabbage tuna pancake **43**
   chicken wings **151**
   corn pakoras **157**
   crunchy noodle potato salad **53**
   loaded garlic bread **131**
   open chicken pie **139**
   toasted tuna chimichangas **119**
meatballs: masala meatballs **19**
   meatball dinner **85**
meatloaf **86**
milk: chai cake **191**
   chocolate pudding **221**
   corndog cake **132**
   croissant berry pudding slices **197**
   fish finger potato bake **78**
   hot chocolate **228**
   rice pudding **34**
mushrooms: kimchi tofu **112**
   steak and mushroom **71**
mustard: mac & cheese **82**

N

noodles: crunchy noodle potato salad **53**
   honey chicken udon **58**
   soba chicken noodles **16**
nori sheets: chicken seaweed kebabs **153**
   orange peppercorn duck breast **89**

O

oats: carrot cake flapjack **188**
onions: air-fried gnocchi **111**
   beef ginger stir-fry **40**

butter bean salmon **77**

Cajun spiced salmon **96**

caramelized onion pasta **12**

cheese & onion potato pie with curry beans **99**

corn pakoras **157**

crab stick fried rice **50**

Creole-style prawns **23**

crunchy noodle potato salad **53**

dumpling salad **54**

fajitas **108**

fish & coconut curry **24**

garlicky onion & yoghurt curry **28**

goat's cheese & onion tart **128**

masala meatballs **19**

mega burgers **115**

oven crab risotto **90**

pan-fried gnocchi **61**

savoury crumpets **66**

shawarma fries **125**

simple dhal **15**

steak and hash browns **116**

onions, crispy fried: meatloaf **86**

orange blossom water: sweet crunchy cannelloni **167**

oranges: orange peppercorn duck breast **89**

sweet crunchy cannelloni **167**

P

pack choi: orange peppercorn duck breast **89**

pak choi: kimchi tofu **112**

pakoras, corn **157**

pancakes: cabbage tuna pancake **43**

pancake nibbles **62**

parsnips: roast chicken dinner **93**

passata: Creole-style prawns **23**

halloumi bake **81**

meatball dinner **85**

pasta: baked feta pasta **74**

caramelized onion pasta **12**

crispy ravioli snack **154**

mac & cheese **82**

messy lasagne **79**

peanuts: fried peanut pie **203**

peas: keema rice **27**

oven crab risotto **90**

pecans: banana cake balls **164**

brown butter pecan coffee cake **182–4**

peppers: cheese-stuffed chicken & mash **102**

corndog cake **132**

Creole-style prawns **23**

fajitas **108**

halloumi bake **81**

pan-fried gnocchi **61**

pesto: cheese loaded flatbread **124**

pickled red cabbage: shawarma fries **125**

pickles: cheese and pickle snack **42**

pies: cheese & onion potato pie with curry beans **99**

fried peanut pie **203**

open chicken pie **139**

pineapple: box pineapple cake **181**

pistachios: chocolate pista scones **218**
    rice pudding **34**
polenta: corndog cake **132**
potatoes see also hash browns: cheese & onion potato pie with curry beans **99**
    fish finger potato bake **78**
    meatloaf **86**
    roast chicken dinner **93**
    steak & wedges **140**
prawns: chilli coconut prawns **105**
    Creole-style prawns **23**
    prawn toasties **65**
pretzels: chocolate shards **222**
puddings: warm cookie dough balls **170**
puddings & sweets: banana cake balls **164**
    chocolate pudding **221**
    golden syrup dumplings **35**
    rice pudding **34**
    sweet crunchy cannelloni **167**
    two-ingredient chocolate mousse **212**

R

raisins: carrot cake flapjack **188**
raspberries: croissant berry pudding slices **197**
ravioli: crispy ravioli snack **154**
red cabbage, pickled: shawarma fries **125**
rice: Cajun spiced salmon **96**
    chicken rice **20**
    crab stick fried rice **50**
    keema rice **27**
    oven crab risotto **90**
    rice pudding **34**
Rice Krispies: crunchy chocolate chip cookies **226**
rice paper: chicken half-moons **47**
    rice paper tteokbokki **31**

S

salads: crunchy noodle potato salad **53**
    dumpling salad **54**
salmon: butter bean salmon **77**
    Cajun spiced salmon **96**
sausages: corndog cake **132**
    frankfurter bacon sarnies **136**
scones, chocolate pista **218**
seaweed see nori sheets
shawarma fries **125**
Shreddies: choco chow **213**
soba chicken noodles **16**
soups: soba chicken noodles **16**
sour cream: messy lasagne **79**
spinach: filo feta squares **57**
    fish & coconut curry **24**
    meatball dinner **85**
    pan-fried gnocchi **61**
spring onions: cabbage tuna pancake **43**
    chicken half-moons **47**
    chicken seaweed kebabs **153**
    honey chicken udon **58**
    loaded garlic bread **131**
    prawn toasties **65**
    toasted tuna chimichangas **119**
sriracha: air-fried gnocchi **111**

cabbage tuna pancake **43**
steak & wedges **140**
steak and hash browns **116**
steak and mushroom **71**
stir-fries: beef ginger stir-fry **40**
    crab stick fried rice **50**
    honey chicken udon **58**
sweet potatoes: baked cod **122**
sweetcorn: beef ginger stir-fry **40**
    corn pakoras **157**
    crab stick fried rice **50**
    halloumi bake **81**
    toasted tuna chimichangas **119**

T

tahini: choco chow **213**
tandoori chicken drums **143**
tarts: fried peanut pie **203**
    goat's cheese & onion tart **128**
tea: chai cake **191**
tofu: kimchi tofu **112**
tomato paste: masala meatballs **19**
    tandoori chicken drums **143**
tomatoes: baked cod **122**
    baked feta pasta **74**
    butter bean salmon **77**
    cheese loaded flatbread **124**
    filo feta squares **57**
    messy lasagne **79**
    oven crab risotto **90**
tortillas: fajitas **108**

toasted tuna chimichangas **119**
tteokbokki, rice paper **31**
tuna: cabbage tuna pancake **43**
    toasted tuna chimichangas **119**
Twix bars: chocolate brownies **208–10**

W

white chocolate: croissant berry pudding slices **197**

Y

yakitori chicken skewers **135**
yoghurt: chocolate pista scones **218**
    corn pakoras **157**
    garlicky onion & yoghurt curry **28**
    shawarma fries **125**
    tandoori chicken drums **143**
    two pots of yoghurt cake **204**
Yorkshire puddings: roast chicken dinner **93**